Around The World

BY TONY TALLARICO

Kidsbooks®

Copyright © 2006 Kidsbooks, LLC, and Tony Tallarico
www.kidsbooks.com

Visit us at www.kidsbooks.com

KARA SEA

YENISEY RIVER

URAL MOUNTAINS

OB RIVER

THE 62 TALLEST MOUNTAINS IN THE WORLD ARE IN ASIA.

AZERBAIJAN

GEORGIA

ARMENIA

BLACK SEA

UZBEKISTAN

KAZAKHSTAN

TAJIKISTAN

CASPIAN SEA

TURKMENISTAN

EUROPE

TURKEY

SYRIA

LEBANON

ISRAEL

IRAQ

IRAN

KUWAIT

AFGHANISTAN

PAKISTAN

JORDAN

PERSIAN GULF

MEDITERRANEAN SEA

DEAD SEA

SAUDI ARABIA

RED SEA

UNITED ARAB EMIRATES

OMAN

AFRICA

ATLANTIC OCEAN

THE HIGHEST (MT. EVEREST) AND THE LOWEST (DEAD SEA) POINTS ON EARTH ARE LOCATED IN ASIA.

THE GOBI DESERT COVERS ABOUT 500,000 SQUARE MILES.

YEMEN

ARABIAN SEA

THE WORLD'S MAJOR RELIGIONS BEGAN IN ASIA.

QATAR

ASIA, AUSTRALIA, AND OCEANIA

THE EARLIEST RECORDED CIVILIZATION AROSE IN THE AREA FROM THE MEDITERRANEAN SEA THROUGH SYRIA AND IRAQ TO THE PERSIAN GULF.

IT'S THAT WAY!

Asia, the largest of the continents, stretches from above the Arctic Circle to below the equator, and from the Ural Mountains in the west to the Pacific Ocean in the east. Asia's lands include some of the coldest, hottest, wettest, and driest places on Earth.

South and east of Asia lie Australia, New Zealand, and many small island nations in the Pacific, most of which lie south of the equator. Together, they form a region that is known as Oceania.

NORTH

WEST

EAST

SOUTH

LEARN ABOUT ASIA, AUSTRALIA, AND OCEANIA AS YOU LOOK FOR THESE FUN ITEMS:

- ❑ Bird
- ❑ Coffeepot
- ❑ Elephant
- ❑ Gold
- ❑ Kangaroo
- ❑ Lobster
- ❑ Mermaid
- ❑ Mountain climber
- ❑ Octopus
- ❑ Oil well
- ❑ Penguin
- ❑ Polar bear
- ❑ Sailboat
- ❑ Telescope

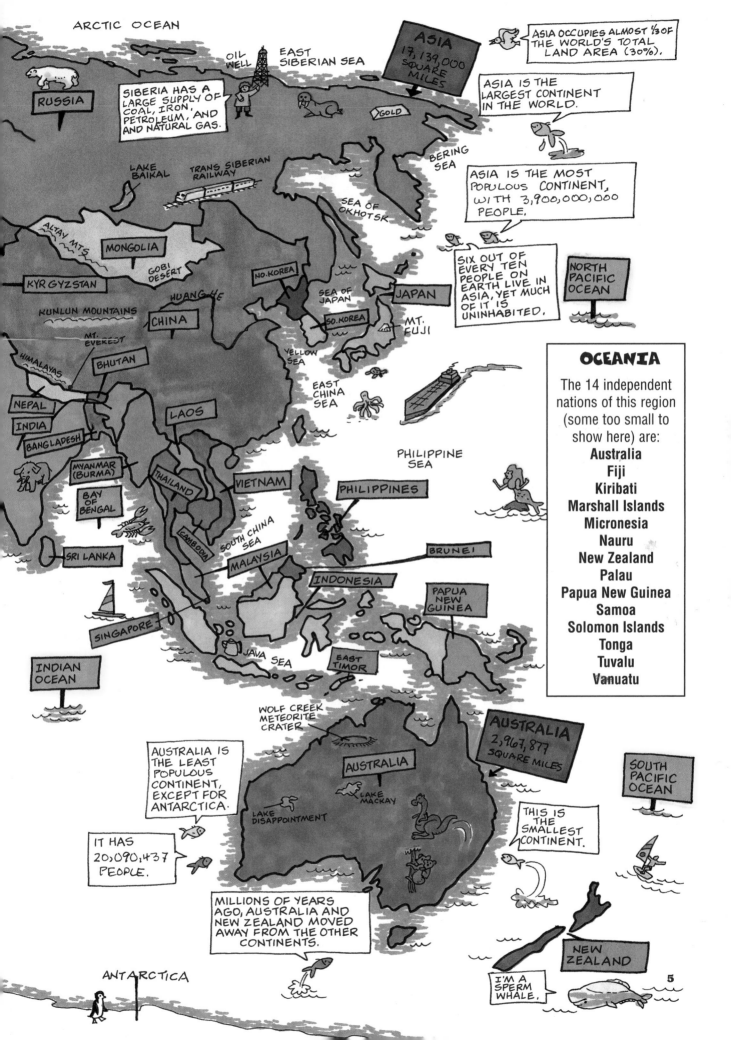

RUSSIA AND ITS NEIGHBORS

Russia, the world's largest country, spans two continents. It covers more than 50 percent of Europe and more than 35 percent of Asia.

Russia used to be part of an even bigger nation called the Soviet Union, which broke apart in 1991. Many of the countries to Russia's south, now independent, also were part of the Soviet Union until 1991.

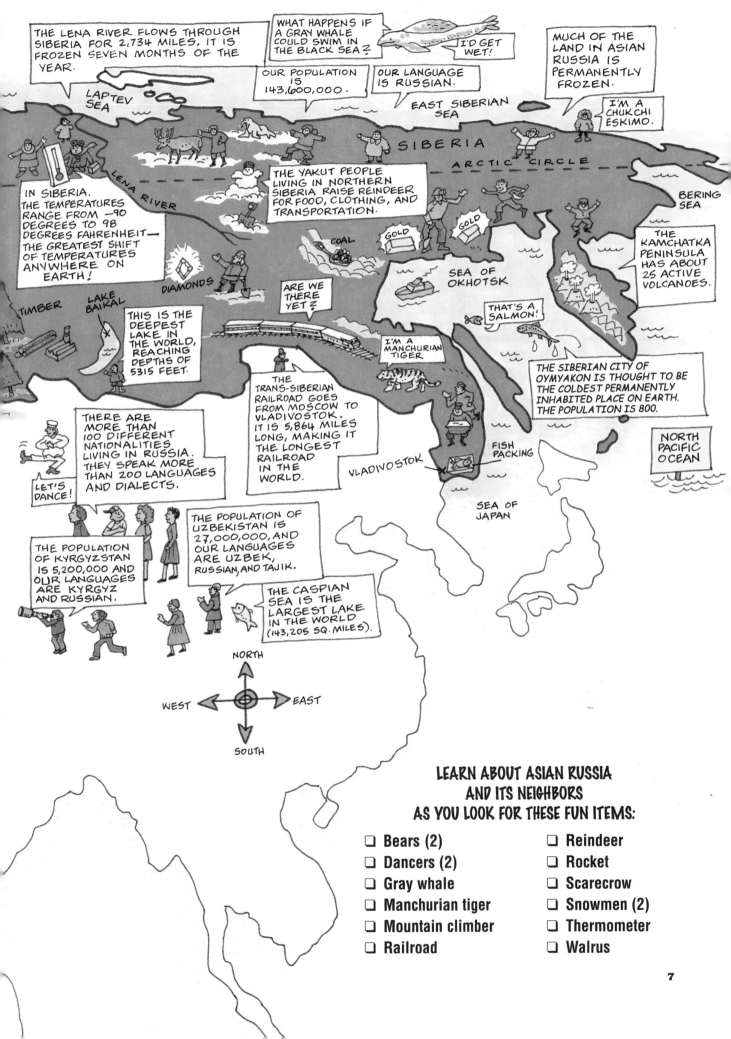

LEARN ABOUT ASIAN RUSSIA
AND ITS NEIGHBORS
AS YOU LOOK FOR THESE FUN ITEMS:

- ❏ Bears (2)
- ❏ Dancers (2)
- ❏ Gray whale
- ❏ Manchurian tiger
- ❏ Mountain climber
- ❏ Railroad
- ❏ Reindeer
- ❏ Rocket
- ❏ Scarecrow
- ❏ Snowmen (2)
- ❏ Thermometer
- ❏ Walrus

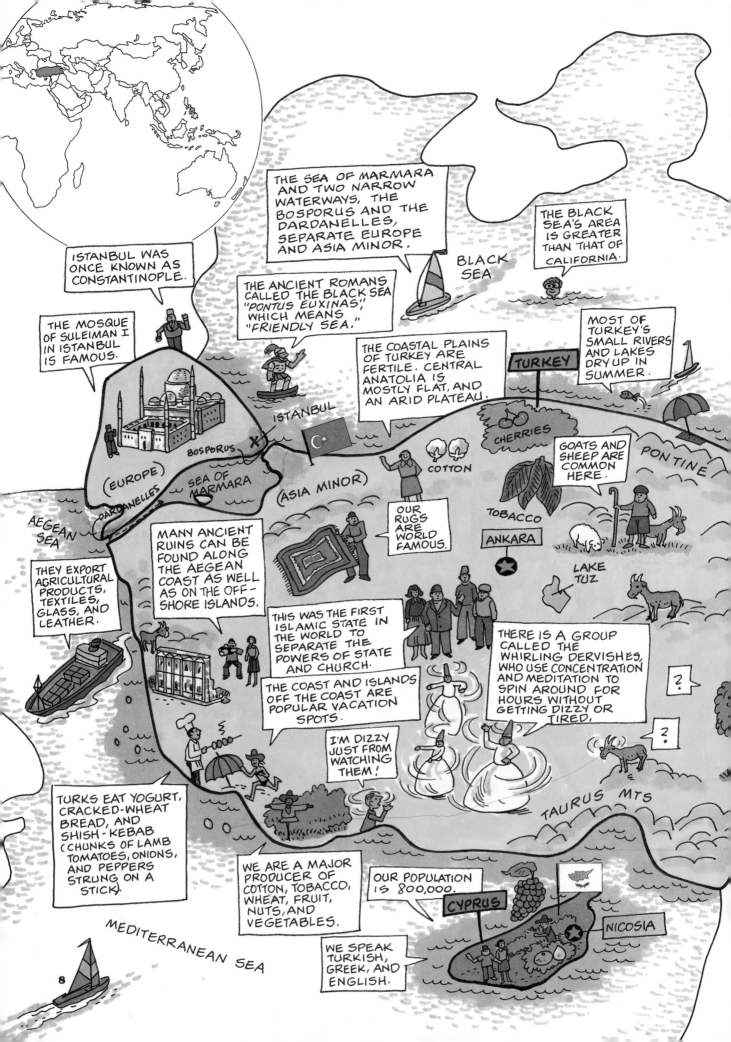

TURKEY AND CYPRUS

Three percent of Turkey's land area lies in Europe. The rest is in Asia, in a region known as Anatolia or Asia Minor. Istanbul, which is Turkey's largest city, is the only city in the world that occupies land on two continents.

Cyprus is only 140 miles long at its longest point, and 60 miles wide at its widest point. It has long been controlled by other nations, and Greece and Turkey both still claim parts of it.

LEARN ABOUT TURKEY AND CYPRUS AS YOU LOOK FOR THESE FUN ITEMS:

- ❑ Apples
- ❑ Ball
- ❑ Bears (3)
- ❑ Book
- ❑ Cook
- ❑ Cowboy
- ❑ Egg
- ❑ Fish
- ❑ Goats (5)
- ❑ Grapes
- ❑ Ibis
- ❑ Ladder
- ❑ Sailboats (3)
- ❑ Shepherd
- ❑ Tea bag
- ❑ Telescope
- ❑ Tin Man
- ❑ Umbrellas (2)

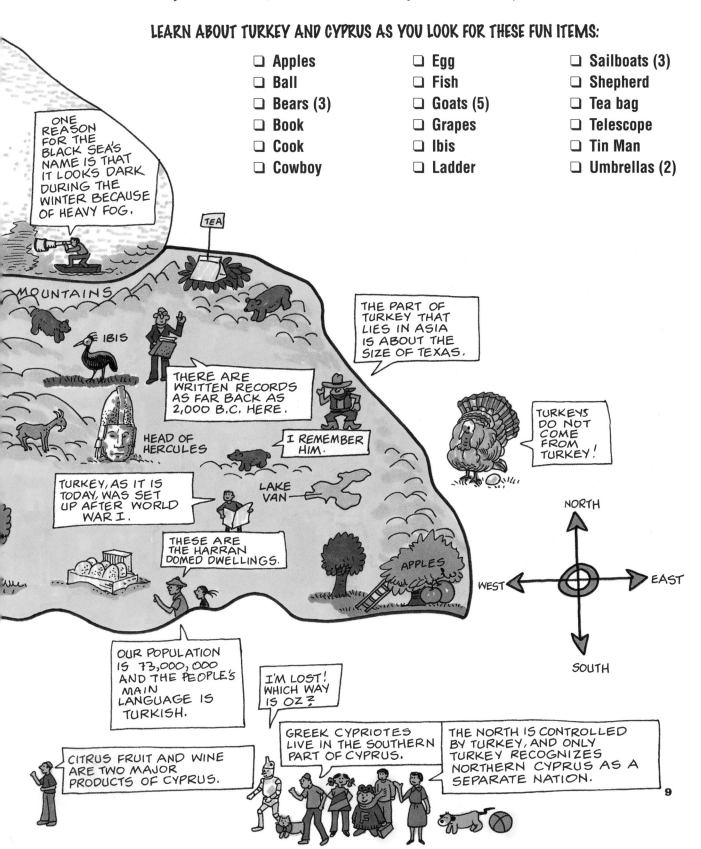

9

THE MIDDLE EAST

This part of Asia, in the area between the Tigris and Euphrates rivers, was one of the first places where civilization was recorded. Towns and communities were thriving here 6,000 years ago. The Arabian Peninsula *(see pp. 12-13)* is also part of the Middle East—a region that has about 75 percent of the world's oil reserves.

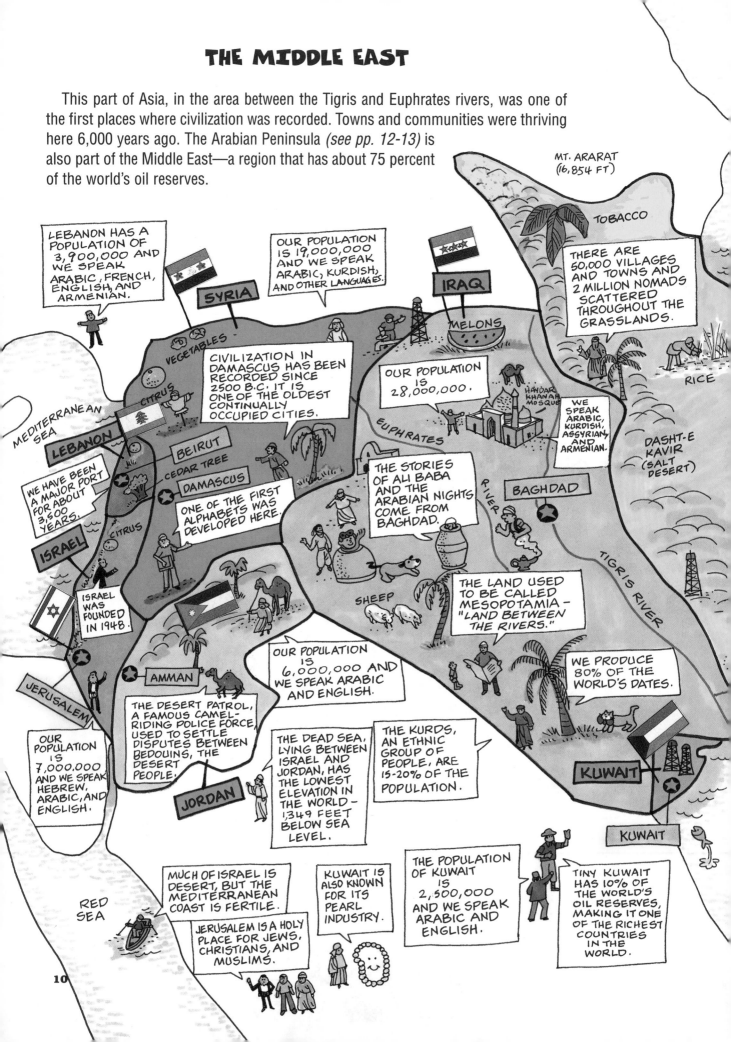

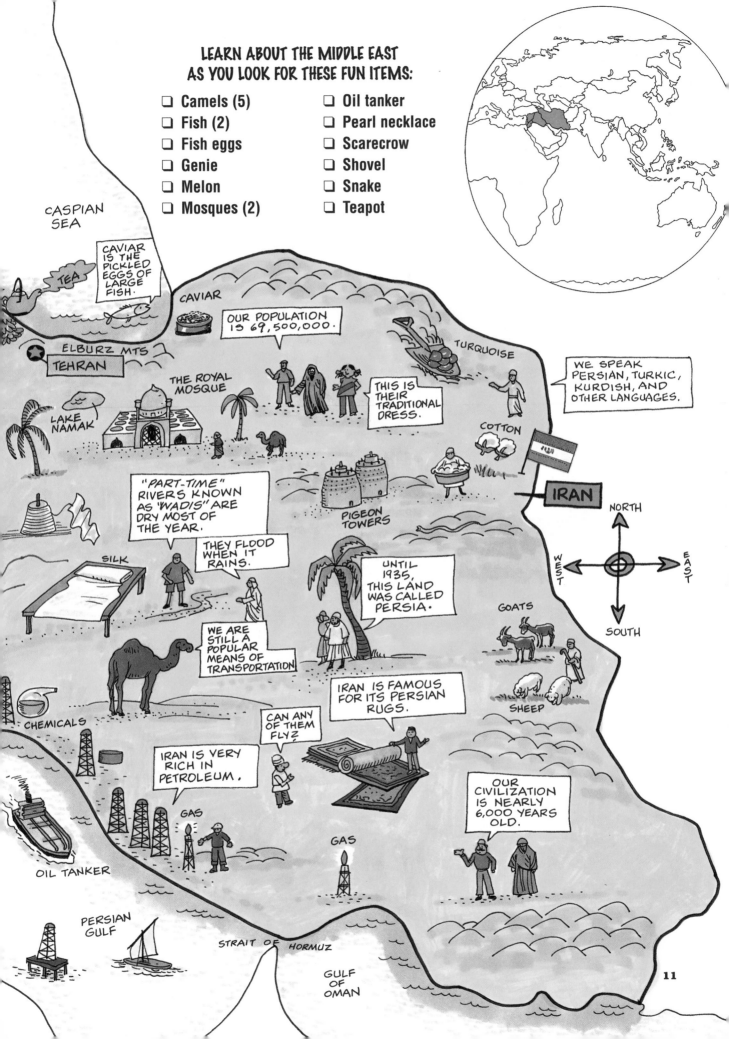

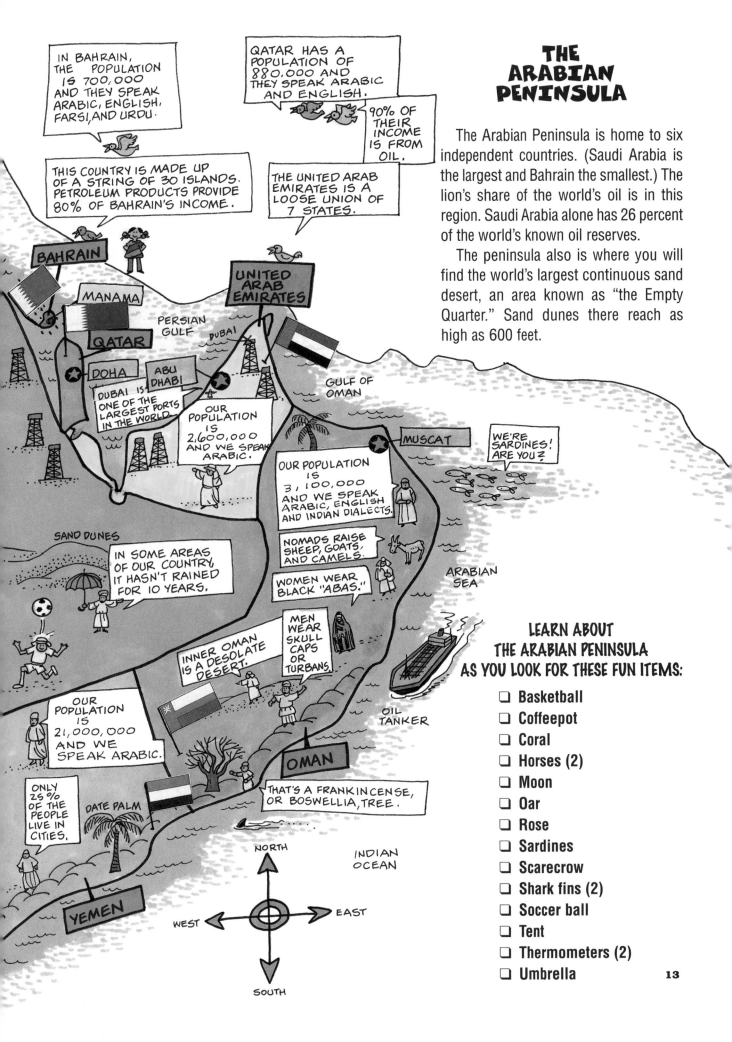

THE ARABIAN PENINSULA

The Arabian Peninsula is home to six independent countries. (Saudi Arabia is the largest and Bahrain the smallest.) The lion's share of the world's oil is in this region. Saudi Arabia alone has 26 percent of the world's known oil reserves.

The peninsula also is where you will find the world's largest continuous sand desert, an area known as "the Empty Quarter." Sand dunes there reach as high as 600 feet.

LEARN ABOUT THE ARABIAN PENINSULA AS YOU LOOK FOR THESE FUN ITEMS:

- ❑ Basketball
- ❑ Coffeepot
- ❑ Coral
- ❑ Horses (2)
- ❑ Moon
- ❑ Oar
- ❑ Rose
- ❑ Sardines
- ❑ Scarecrow
- ❑ Shark fins (2)
- ❑ Soccer ball
- ❑ Tent
- ❑ Thermometers (2)
- ❑ Umbrella

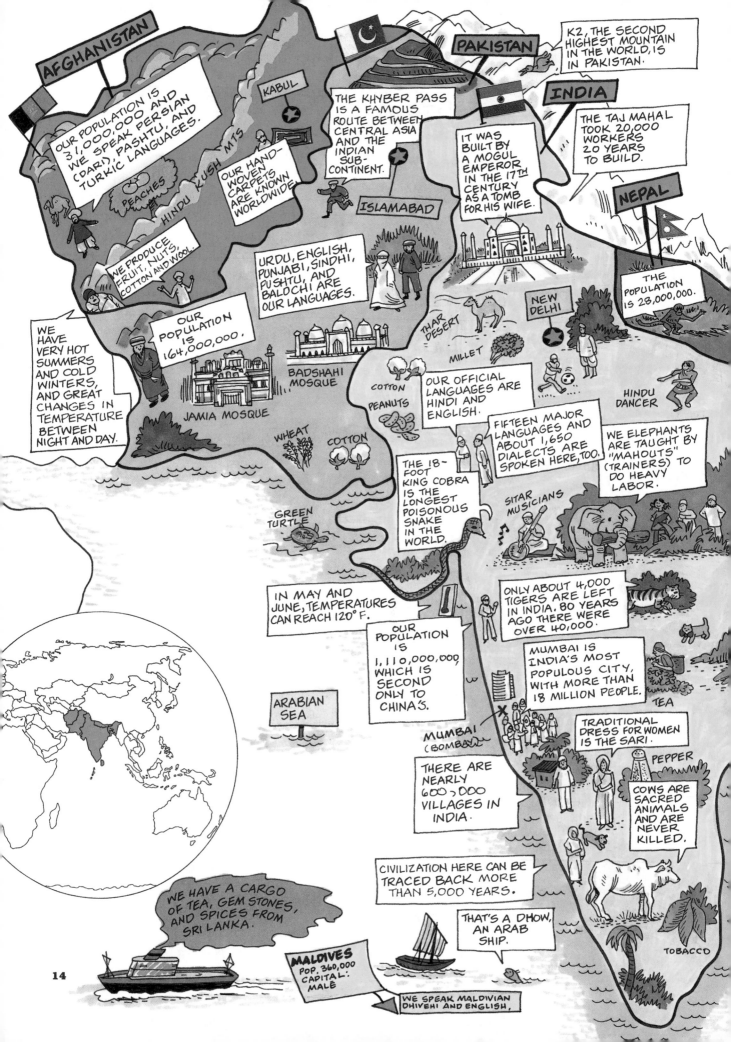

THE INDIAN SUBCONTINENT

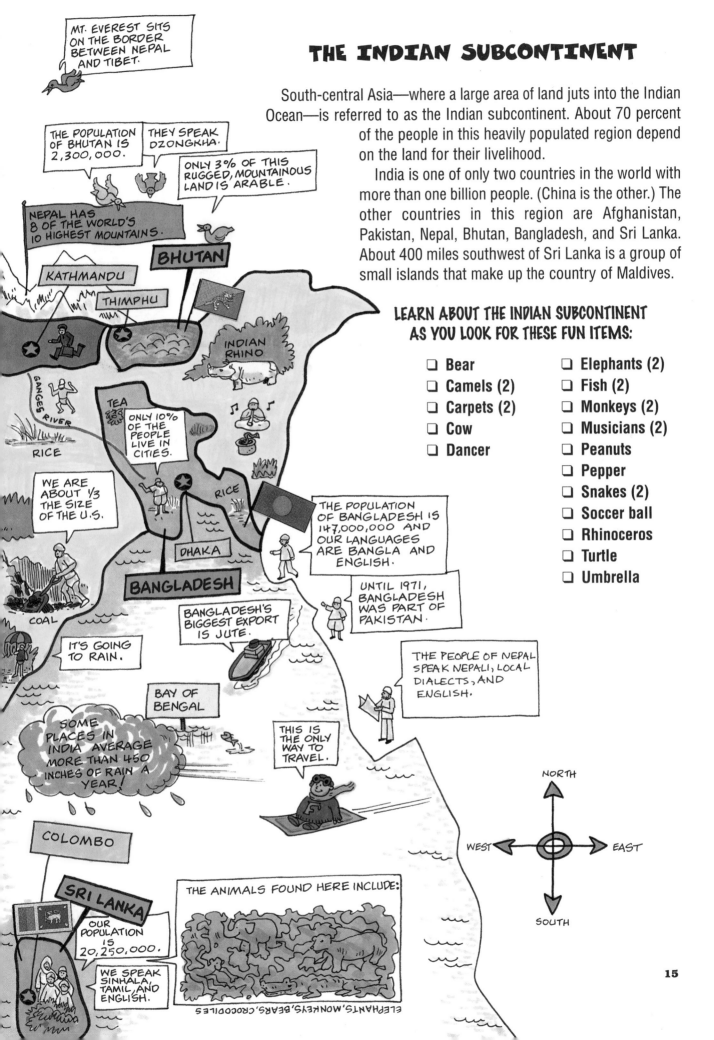

MT. EVEREST SITS ON THE BORDER BETWEEN NEPAL AND TIBET.

South-central Asia—where a large area of land juts into the Indian Ocean—is referred to as the Indian subcontinent. About 70 percent of the people in this heavily populated region depend on the land for their livelihood.

India is one of only two countries in the world with more than one billion people. (China is the other.) The other countries in this region are Afghanistan, Pakistan, Nepal, Bhutan, Bangladesh, and Sri Lanka. About 400 miles southwest of Sri Lanka is a group of small islands that make up the country of Maldives.

THE POPULATION OF BHUTAN IS 2,300,000.

THEY SPEAK DZONGKHA.

ONLY 3% OF THIS RUGGED, MOUNTAINOUS LAND IS ARABLE.

NEPAL HAS 8 OF THE WORLD'S 10 HIGHEST MOUNTAINS.

BHUTAN

KATHMANDU

THIMPHU

INDIAN RHINO

GANGES RIVER

RICE

TEA

ONLY 10% OF THE PEOPLE LIVE IN CITIES.

WE ARE ABOUT ⅓ THE SIZE OF THE U.S.

RICE

DHAKA

BANGLADESH

COAL

THE POPULATION OF BANGLADESH IS 147,000,000 AND OUR LANGUAGES ARE BANGLA AND ENGLISH.

UNTIL 1971, BANGLADESH WAS PART OF PAKISTAN.

BANGLADESH'S BIGGEST EXPORT IS JUTE.

IT'S GOING TO RAIN.

BAY OF BENGAL

THE PEOPLE OF NEPAL SPEAK NEPALI, LOCAL DIALECTS, AND ENGLISH.

SOME PLACES IN INDIA AVERAGE MORE THAN 450 INCHES OF RAIN A YEAR!

THIS IS THE ONLY WAY TO TRAVEL.

COLOMBO

NORTH

WEST

EAST

SOUTH

SRI LANKA

OUR POPULATION IS 20,250,000.

WE SPEAK SINHALA, TAMIL, AND ENGLISH.

THE ANIMALS FOUND HERE INCLUDE:

ELEPHANTS, MONKEYS, BEARS, CROCODILES

LEARN ABOUT THE INDIAN SUBCONTINENT AS YOU LOOK FOR THESE FUN ITEMS:

- ❏ Bear
- ❏ Camels (2)
- ❏ Carpets (2)
- ❏ Cow
- ❏ Dancer
- ❏ Elephants (2)
- ❏ Fish (2)
- ❏ Monkeys (2)
- ❏ Musicians (2)
- ❏ Peanuts
- ❏ Pepper
- ❏ Snakes (2)
- ❏ Soccer ball
- ❏ Rhinoceros
- ❏ Turtle
- ❏ Umbrella

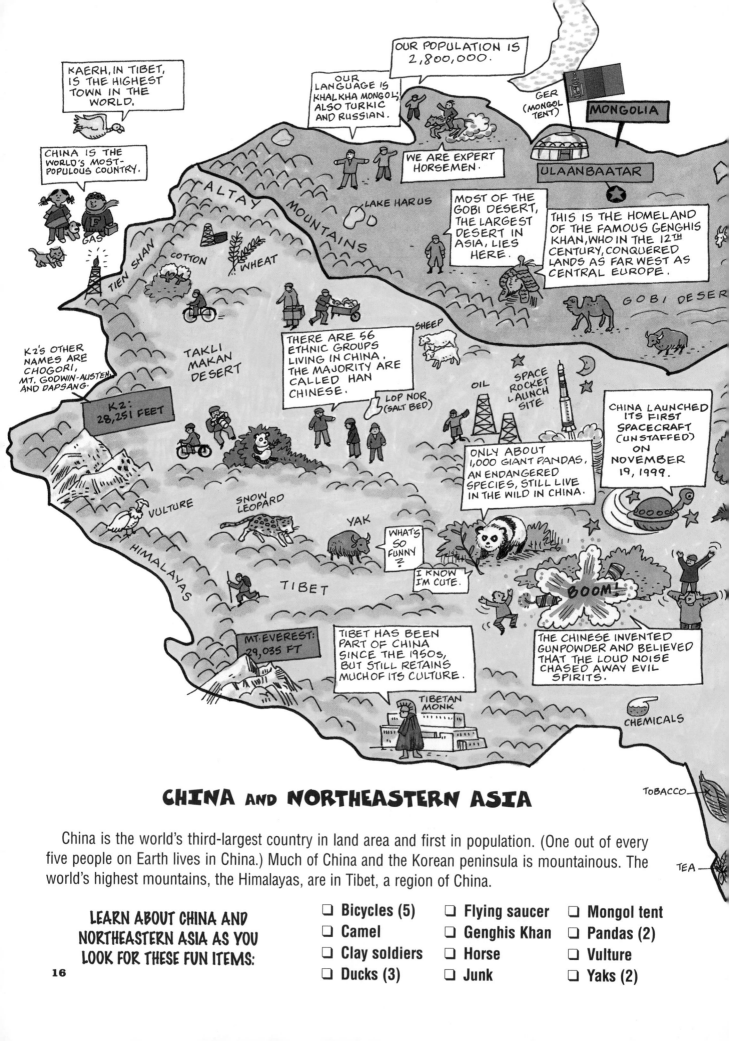

CHINA AND NORTHEASTERN ASIA

China is the world's third-largest country in land area and first in population. (One out of every five people on Earth lives in China.) Much of China and the Korean peninsula is mountainous. The world's highest mountains, the Himalayas, are in Tibet, a region of China.

LEARN ABOUT CHINA AND NORTHEASTERN ASIA AS YOU LOOK FOR THESE FUN ITEMS:

☐ Bicycles (5)   ☐ Flying saucer   ☐ Mongol tent
☐ Camel   ☐ Genghis Khan   ☐ Pandas (2)
☐ Clay soldiers   ☐ Horse   ☐ Vulture
☐ Ducks (3)   ☐ Junk   ☐ Yaks (2)

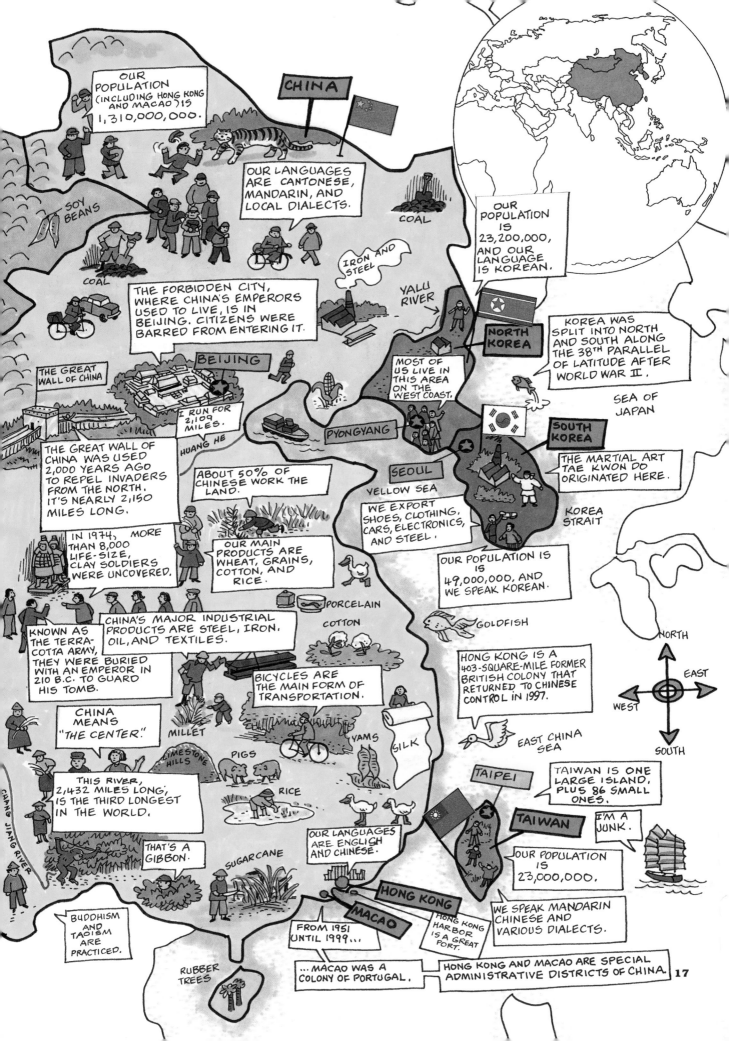

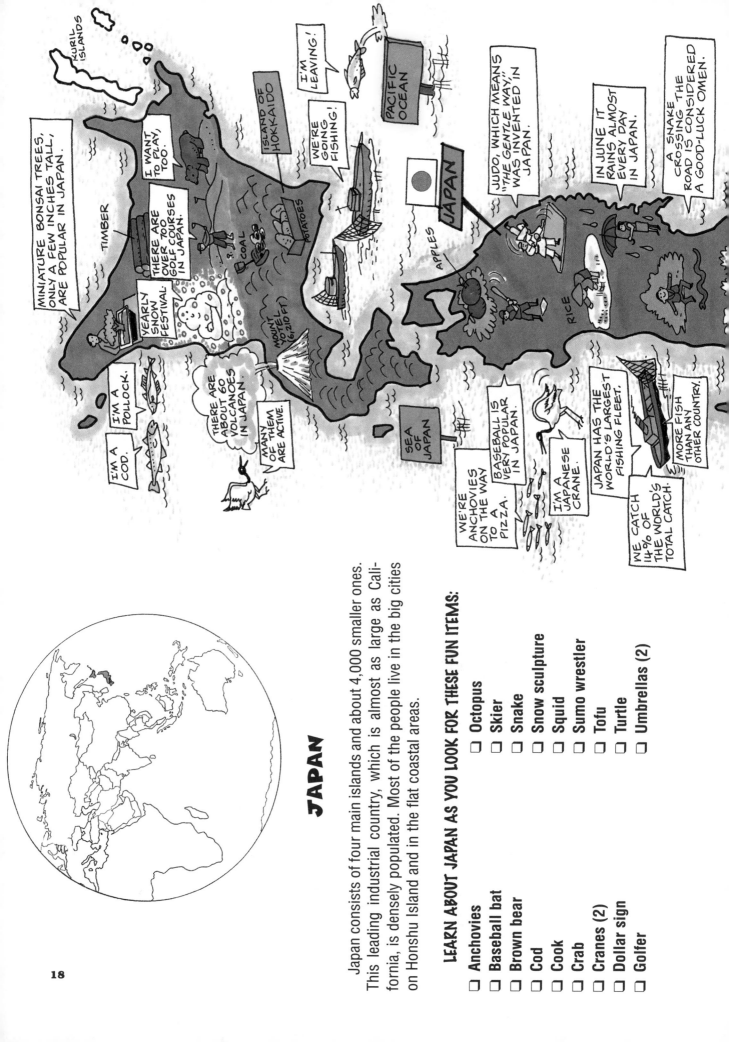

JAPAN

Japan consists of four main islands and about 4,000 smaller ones. This leading industrial country, which is almost as large as California, is densely populated. Most of the people live in the big cities on Honshu Island and in the flat coastal areas.

LEARN ABOUT JAPAN AS YOU LOOK FOR THESE FUN ITEMS:

- ☐ Anchovies
- ☐ Baseball bat
- ☐ Brown bear
- ☐ Cod
- ☐ Cook
- ☐ Crab
- ☐ Cranes (2)
- ☐ Dollar sign
- ☐ Golfer
- ☐ Octopus
- ☐ Skier
- ☐ Snake
- ☐ Snow sculpture
- ☐ Squid
- ☐ Sumo wrestler
- ☐ Tofu
- ☐ Turtle
- ☐ Umbrellas (2)

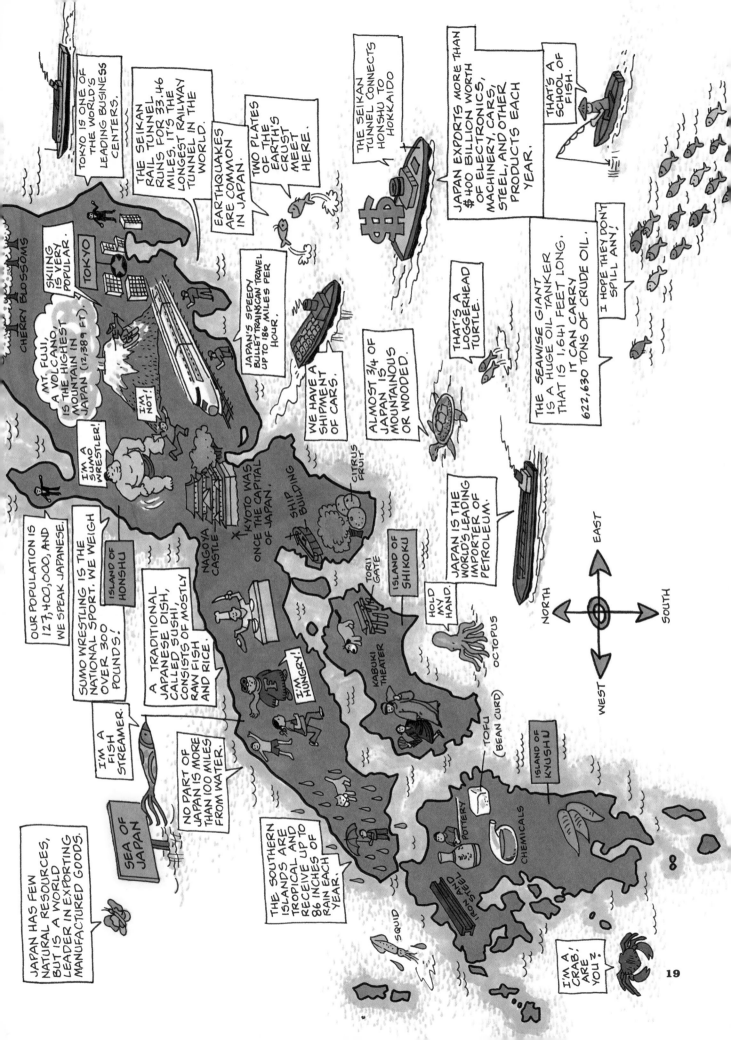

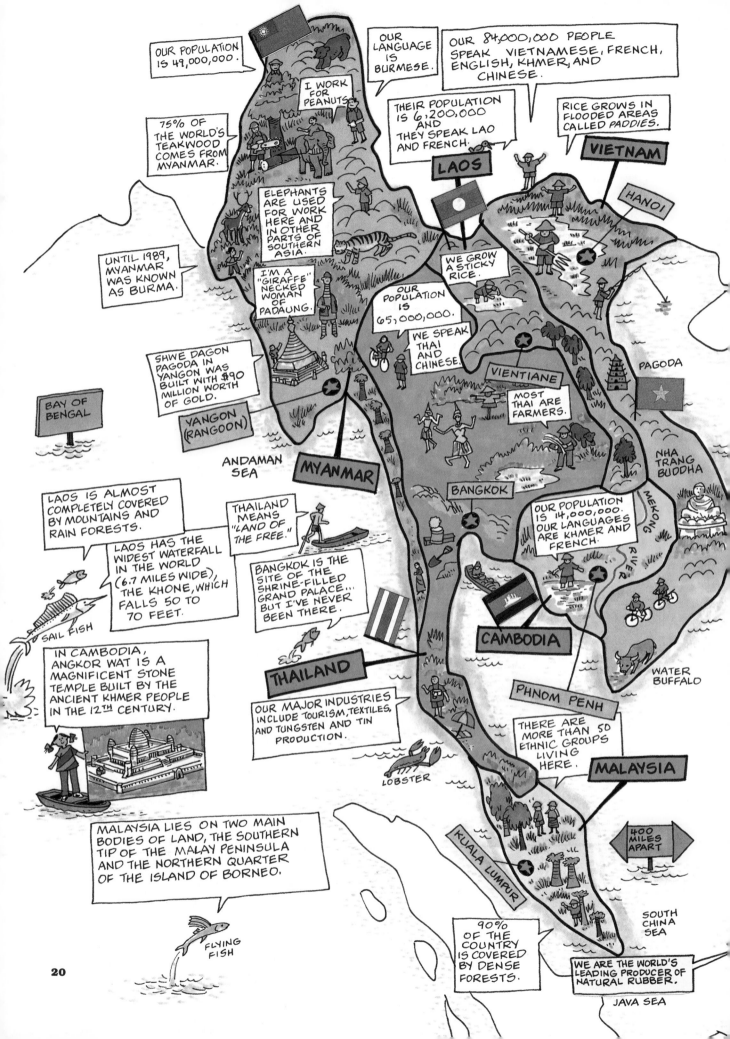

SOUTHEAST ASIA

This region is close to the equator, giving it a tropical climate with periods of heavy rainfall. Dense jungles or tropical rain forests cover much of the area, which has three main types of landscape: mountains, plains, or high, flat areas called plateaus. Most people here live near water—oceans, seas, or mighty rivers. Many Southeast Asians use the waterways for irrigating farmland, fishing, and transportation.

LEARN ABOUT SOUTHEAST ASIA
AS YOU LOOK FOR THESE FUN ITEMS:

- ❑ Brown bears (2)
- ❑ Cyclists (3)
- ❑ Dancers
- ❑ Deer
- ❑ Elephant
- ❑ Fisherman
- ❑ Flying fish
- ❑ "Giraffe" necked woman
- ❑ Lobster
- ❑ Pitchfork
- ❑ Scarecrow
- ❑ Tiger
- ❑ Umbrellas (2)

MORE THAN 60% OF THE VIETNAMESE FARM OR FISH.

SOUTH CHINA SEA

VIETNAM HAS A VERY TROPICAL CLIMATE.

DURING THE MONSOON SEASON, STRONG WINDS AND HEAVY RAINS ARE COMMON, ESPECIALLY IN THE SOUTHERN REGIONS.

THEY HAVE ONLY TWO SEASONS - A WET, HOT SUMMER AND A COOL WINTER.

THE HEART OF CAMBODIA IS THE RIVER BASIN WATERED BY THE MEKONG RIVER.

THE MEKONG RIVER CREATES FERTILE FARMING AREAS WHERE MAINLY RICE AND CORN ARE GROWN.

NORTH
WEST — EAST
SOUTH

MALAYSIA

BANDAR SERI BEGAWAN

WE MAKE A BEAUTIFUL HANDWOVEN CLOTH WITH GOLD AND SILVER THREADS.

THE POPULATION OF BRUNEI IS 400,000. THEY SPEAK MALAY, CHINESE AND ENGLISH.

BRUNEI

BATIK IS A WAY OF PRINTING FABRIC HERE.

THE WORLD'S LARGEST CAVE CHAMBER IS IN SARAWAK, MALAYSIA. IT'S LARGE ENOUGH TO HOLD ABOUT 7,500 BUSES.

THE POPULATION OF MALAYSIA IS 25,000,000 AND THEY SPEAK BAHASA MALAYSIA AND OTHER LANGUAGES.

BORNEO

ARE WE THERE, YET?

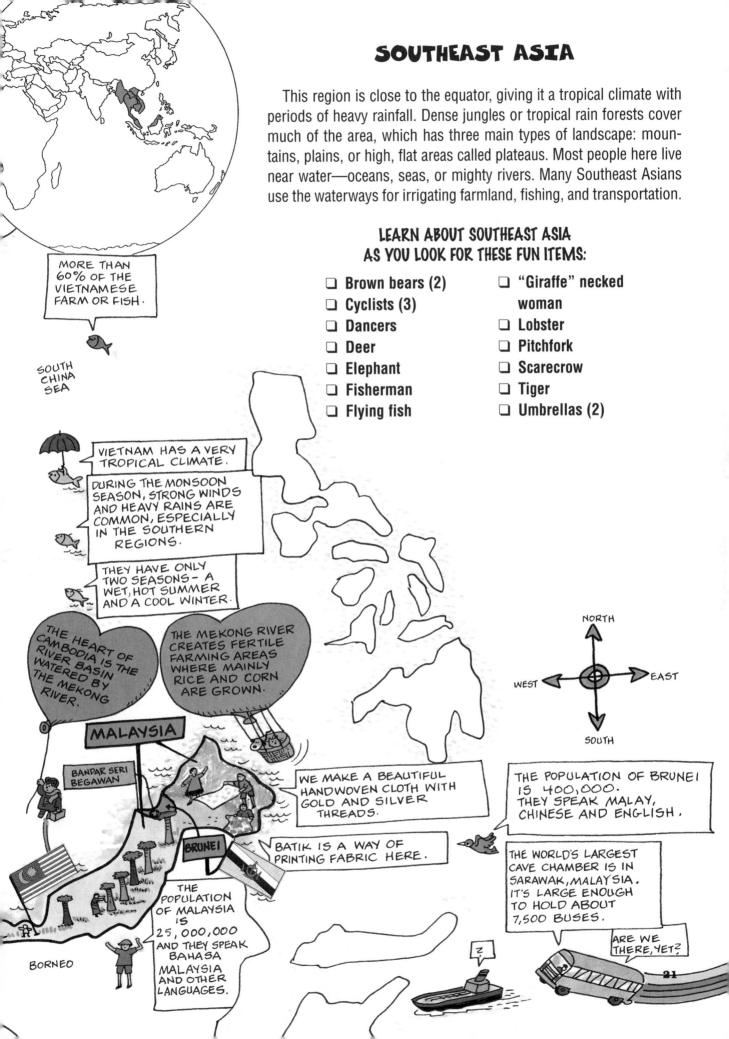

21

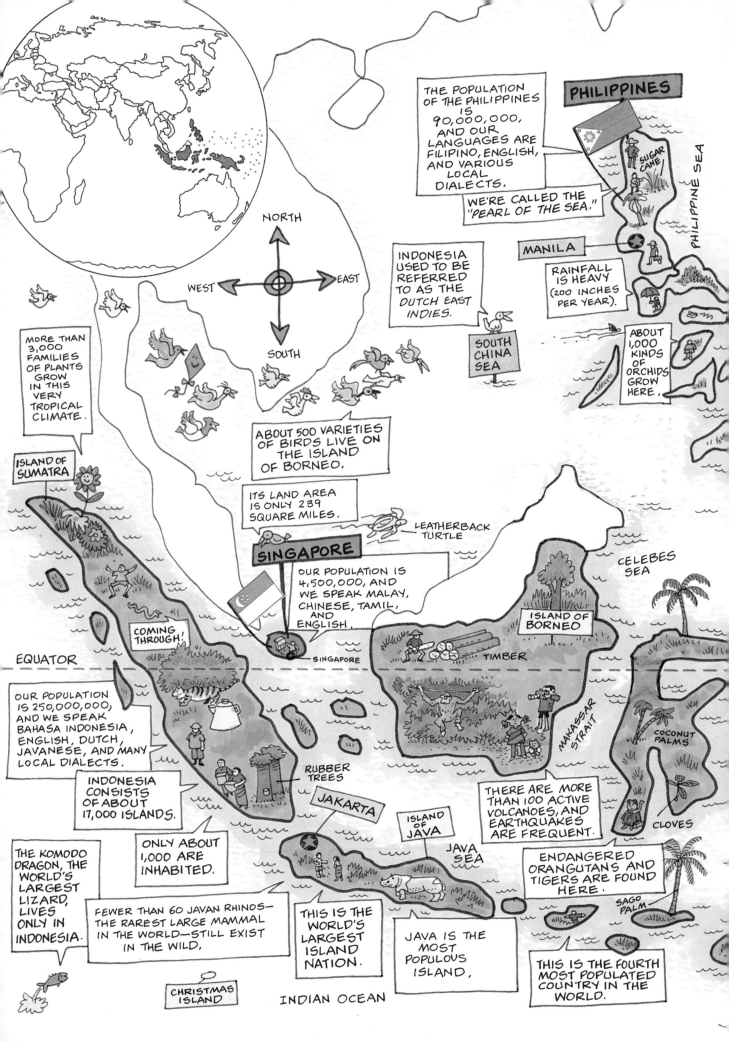

INDONESIA AND PACIFIC ISLAND NATIONS

Indonesia, Singapore, the Philippines, and East Timor are part of Asia. Papua New Guinea and many small island nations scattered in this area of the Pacific Ocean are part of a region called Oceania. *(See p. 5 for a list of all the countries of Oceania.)* Most of this area has a hot, wet, tropical climate.

LEARN ABOUT INDONESIA AND PACIFIC ISLAND NATIONS AS YOU LOOK FOR THESE FUN ITEMS:

- ☐ Airplane
- ☐ Coffeepot
- ☐ Kite
- ☐ Orangutan
- ☐ Photographer
- ☐ Rhinoceros
- ☐ Shark fins (4)
- ☐ Tiger
- ☐ Tree kangaroo
- ☐ Turtle
- ☐ Tuna
- ☐ Volcanoes (2)

THE CLIMATE IS HOT AND HUMID.

OVER 80° IS THE AVERAGE TEMPERATURE.

THERE ARE OVER 7,000 ISLANDS IN THE PHILIPPINES. MOST OF THE PEOPLE LIVE ON THESE 11 ISLANDS.

BONIN ISLANDS (JAPAN)

OF ABOUT 25,000 ISLANDS IN THE PACIFIC OCEAN, ONLY A FEW THOUSAND ARE INHABITED.

WAKE ISLAND (U.S.)

NORTH PACIFIC OCEAN

NORTHERN MARIANA ISLANDS (U.S.)

MARSHALL ISLANDS

SOME OF THE PACIFIC ISLANDS MAKE UP NINE INDEPENDENT COUNTRIES.

PALAU

MANY OTHER ISLANDS ARE GOVERNED BY COUNTRIES SUCH AS THE U.S., GREAT BRITAIN, AND FRANCE.

VOLCANIC ERUPTIONS ARE COMMON. THESE ISLANDS ARE ACTUALLY THE TOPS OF MOUNTAINS THAT ARE STILL FORMING.

MICRONESIA

SOME OF THE ISLANDS ARE THE TIPS OF MOUNTAINS OR VOLCANOES, OTHERS ARE MADE UP OF CORAL.

I'M A PEARL OYSTER.

KIRIBATI

EQUATOR

OUR POPULATION IS 5,600,000, AND OUR LANGUAGES ARE ENGLISH, PIDGIN ENGLISH, MOTU, AND MANY OTHERS.

MOLUCCA SEA

INDONESIA

PAPUA NEW GUINEA

RAINFALL IS OVER 100 INCHES ANNUALLY.

HALF THE ISLAND BELONGS TO INDONESIA.

BISMARCK SEA

TREE KANGAROO

BANDA SEA

INDONESIA'S MAIN EXPORTS ARE OIL, TIMBER, RUBBER AND COFFEE.

MT. WILHELM (14,790 FT)

TUVALU

SOLOMON ISLANDS

EAST TIMOR

EAST TIMOR'S LANGUAGES ARE TETUM, PORTUGUESE, INDONESIAN, ENGLISH, AND OTHERS.

VANUATU

PORT MORESBY

EAST TIMOR— THE WORLD'S NEWEST COUNTRY —BECAME INDEPENDENT IN 2002.

FIJI

EAST TIMOR'S POPULATION IS 1,050,000.

ARAFURA SEA

CORAL SEA IS. (AUS)

23

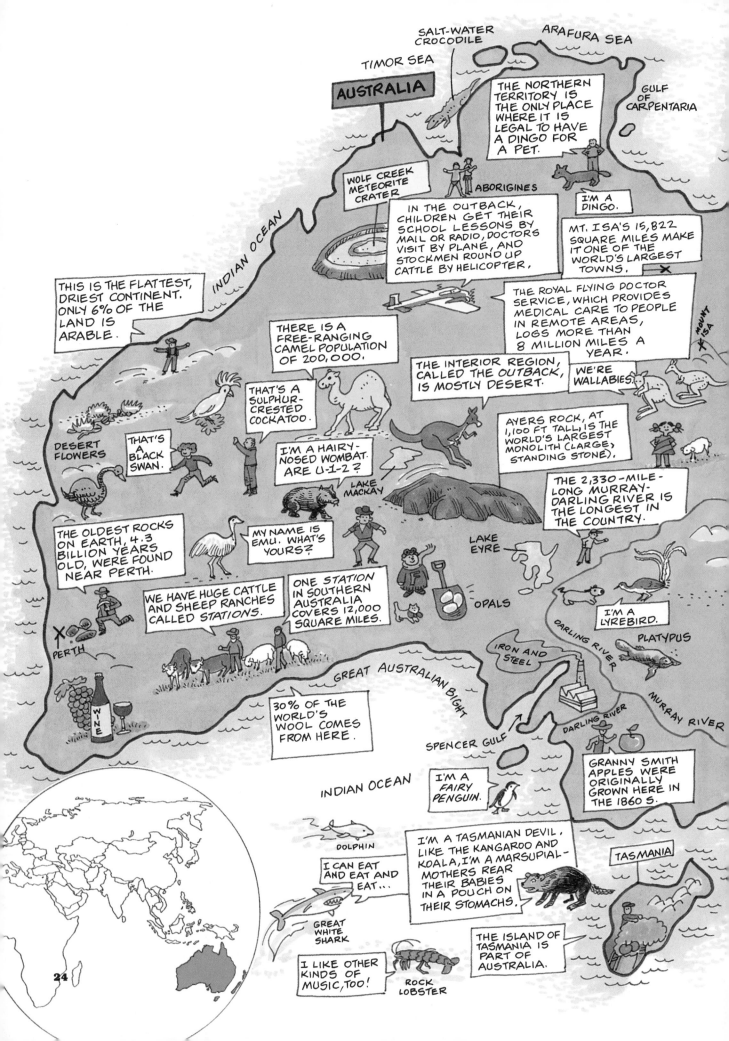

SALT-WATER CROCODILE

ARAFURA SEA

TIMOR SEA

AUSTRALIA

THE NORTHERN TERRITORY IS THE ONLY PLACE WHERE IT IS LEGAL TO HAVE A DINGO FOR A PET.

GULF OF CARPENTARIA

WOLF CREEK METEORITE CRATER

ABORIGINES

I'M A DINGO.

IN THE OUTBACK, CHILDREN GET THEIR SCHOOL LESSONS BY MAIL OR RADIO, DOCTORS VISIT BY PLANE, AND STOCKMEN ROUND UP CATTLE BY HELICOPTER.

MT. ISA'S 15,822 SQUARE MILES MAKE IT ONE OF THE WORLD'S LARGEST TOWNS.

INDIAN OCEAN

THIS IS THE FLATTEST, DRIEST CONTINENT. ONLY 6% OF THE LAND IS ARABLE.

THE ROYAL FLYING DOCTOR SERVICE, WHICH PROVIDES MEDICAL CARE TO PEOPLE IN REMOTE AREAS, LOGS MORE THAN 8 MILLION MILES A YEAR.

MOUNT ISA

THERE IS A FREE-RANGING CAMEL POPULATION OF 200,000.

THE INTERIOR REGION, CALLED THE OUTBACK, IS MOSTLY DESERT.

WE'RE WALLABIES.

THAT'S A SULPHUR-CRESTED COCKATOO.

AYERS ROCK, AT 1,100 FT TALL, IS THE WORLD'S LARGEST MONOLITH (LARGE STANDING STONE).

DESERT FLOWERS

THAT'S A BLACK SWAN.

I'M A HAIRY-NOSED WOMBAT. ARE U-1-2?

LAKE MACKAY

THE 2,330-MILE-LONG MURRAY-DARLING RIVER IS THE LONGEST IN THE COUNTRY.

THE OLDEST ROCKS ON EARTH, 4.3 BILLION YEARS OLD, WERE FOUND NEAR PERTH.

MY NAME IS EMU. WHAT'S YOURS?

LAKE EYRE

WE HAVE HUGE CATTLE AND SHEEP RANCHES CALLED STATIONS.

ONE STATION IN SOUTHERN AUSTRALIA COVERS 12,000 SQUARE MILES.

OPALS

I'M A LYREBIRD.

DARLING RIVER

PLATYPUS

PERTH

IRON AND STEEL

WINE

GREAT AUSTRALIAN BIGHT

DARLING RIVER

MURRAY RIVER

30% OF THE WORLD'S WOOL COMES FROM HERE.

SPENCER GULF

GRANNY SMITH APPLES WERE ORIGINALLY GROWN HERE IN THE 1860S.

INDIAN OCEAN

I'M A FAIRY PENGUIN.

DOLPHIN

I CAN EAT AND EAT AND EAT...

I'M A TASMANIAN DEVIL, LIKE THE KANGAROO AND KOALA, I'M A MARSUPIAL—MOTHERS REAR THEIR BABIES IN A POUCH ON THEIR STOMACHS.

TASMANIA

GREAT WHITE SHARK

THE ISLAND OF TASMANIA IS PART OF AUSTRALIA.

I LIKE OTHER KINDS OF MUSIC, TOO!

ROCK LOBSTER

24

AUSTRALIA AND NEW ZEALAND

Australia is the only country that is also a continent. Its nickname, Down Under, comes from the fact that the entire continent lies south of the equator.

Millions of years ago, Australia broke off from the other continents. Its first settlers, called Aborigines *(AB-uh-RIJ-uh-neez)*, arrived about 40,000 years ago, from islands in the Pacific Ocean. (*Ab origine* means "from the beginning.") Their descendants still live in Australia today.

New Zealand lies about 1,000 miles southeast of Australia. Both countries are in a region called Oceania.

LEARN ABOUT AUSTRALIA AND NEW ZEALAND AS YOU LOOK FOR THESE FUN ITEMS:

- ❑ Banana
- ❑ Camel
- ❑ Cockatoo
- ❑ Emu
- ❑ Kangaroo
- ❑ Koalas (2)
- ❑ Lyrebird
- ❑ Penguin
- ❑ Platypus
- ❑ Sharks (2)
- ❑ Skier
- ❑ Surfers (2)
- ❑ Swan
- ❑ Tasmanian devil
- ❑ Volcano
- ❑ Wallabies (2)
- ❑ Wombat

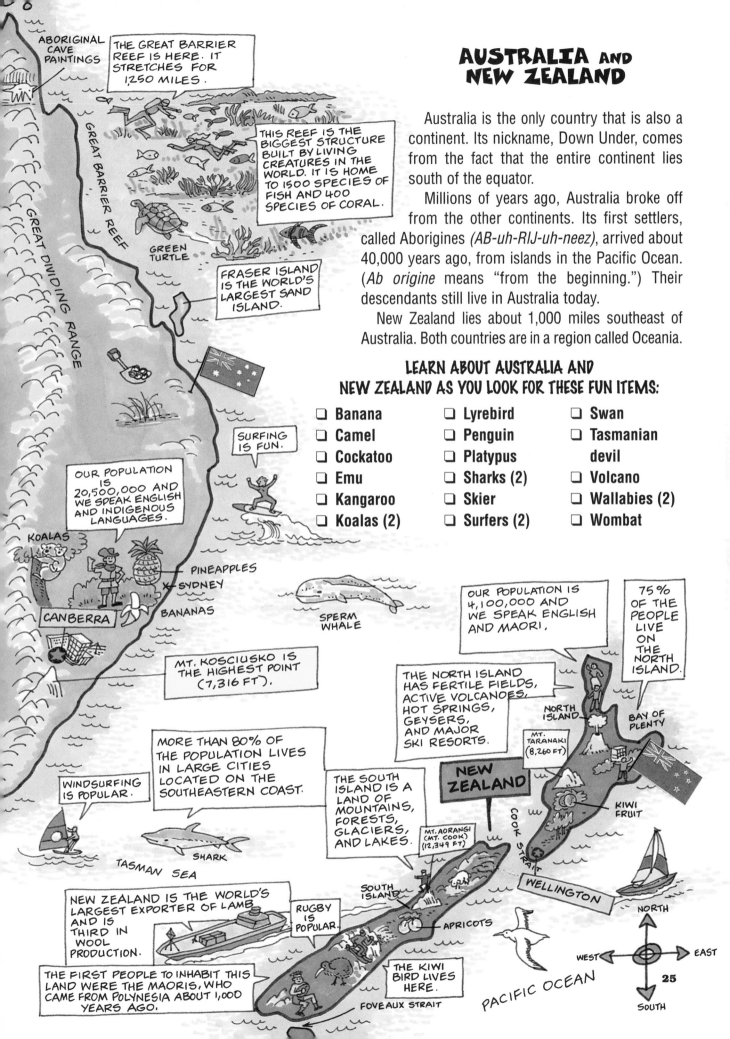

ABORIGINAL CAVE PAINTINGS

THE GREAT BARRIER REEF IS HERE. IT STRETCHES FOR 1,250 MILES.

GREAT BARRIER REEF

THIS REEF IS THE BIGGEST STRUCTURE BUILT BY LIVING CREATURES IN THE WORLD. IT IS HOME TO 1500 SPECIES OF FISH AND 400 SPECIES OF CORAL.

GREEN TURTLE

GREAT DIVIDING RANGE

FRASER ISLAND IS THE WORLD'S LARGEST SAND ISLAND.

SURFING IS FUN.

OUR POPULATION IS 20,500,000 AND WE SPEAK ENGLISH AND INDIGENOUS LANGUAGES.

KOALAS

PINEAPPLES

SYDNEY

CANBERRA

BANANAS

SPERM WHALE

MT. KOSCIUSKO IS THE HIGHEST POINT (7,316 FT).

OUR POPULATION IS 4,100,000 AND WE SPEAK ENGLISH AND MAORI.

75% OF THE PEOPLE LIVE ON THE NORTH ISLAND.

THE NORTH ISLAND HAS FERTILE FIELDS, ACTIVE VOLCANOES, HOT SPRINGS, GEYSERS, AND MAJOR SKI RESORTS.

NORTH ISLAND

MT. TARANAKI (8,260 FT)

BAY OF PLENTY

NEW ZEALAND

KIWI FRUIT

MORE THAN 80% OF THE POPULATION LIVES IN LARGE CITIES LOCATED ON THE SOUTHEASTERN COAST.

THE SOUTH ISLAND IS A LAND OF MOUNTAINS, FORESTS, GLACIERS, AND LAKES.

MT. AORANGI (MT. COOK) (12,349 FT)

WINDSURFING IS POPULAR.

COOK STRAIT

WELLINGTON

SHARK

TASMAN SEA

NEW ZEALAND IS THE WORLD'S LARGEST EXPORTER OF LAMB AND IS THIRD IN WOOL PRODUCTION.

RUGBY IS POPULAR.

SOUTH ISLAND

APRICOTS

THE FIRST PEOPLE TO INHABIT THIS LAND WERE THE MAORIS, WHO CAME FROM POLYNESIA ABOUT 1,000 YEARS AGO.

THE KIWI BIRD LIVES HERE.

FOVEAUX STRAIT

NORTH

WEST — EAST

SOUTH

PACIFIC OCEAN

25

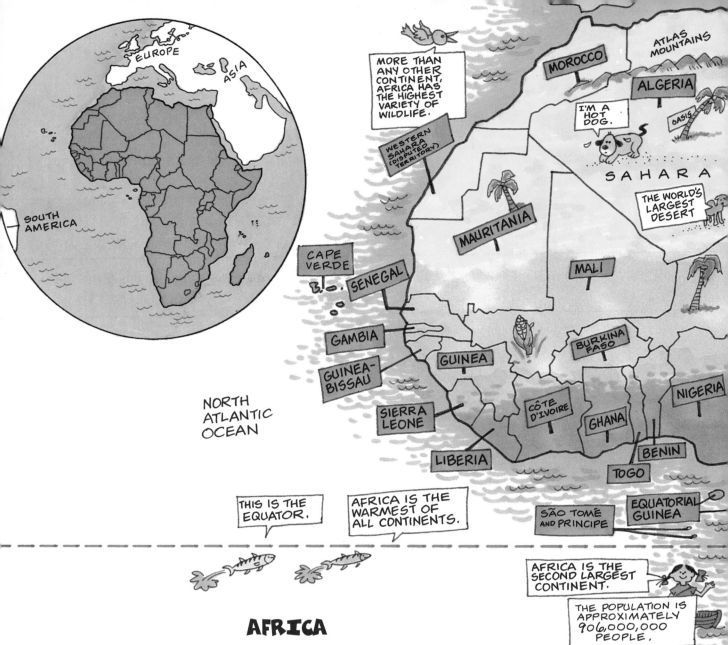

AFRICA

Once an unexplored and mysterious place to Europeans, Africa was known as the "Dark Continent." By the 19th century, European powers influenced or controlled much of Africa. However, starting in the late 1950s, country after country in Africa achieved its independence. The continent now is home to 53 independent nations. Africa's newest country, Eritrea, became independent in 1993, when it split from Ethiopia.

LEARN ABOUT AFRICA AS YOU LOOK FOR THESE FUN ITEMS:

- ❏ Atlas Mountains
- ❏ Butterfly
- ❏ Cape of Good Hope
- ❏ Elephant
- ❏ Gold bar
- ❏ Indian Ocean

- ❏ Mount Kilimanjaro
- ❏ Nile River
- ❏ Oil wells (2)
- ❏ Palm trees (4)
- ❏ Pyramid
- ❏ Rain cloud

- ❏ Rhinoceros
- ❏ Sea horse
- ❏ Sheep (2)
- ❏ Suez Canal
- ❏ Umbrella
- ❏ Zebra

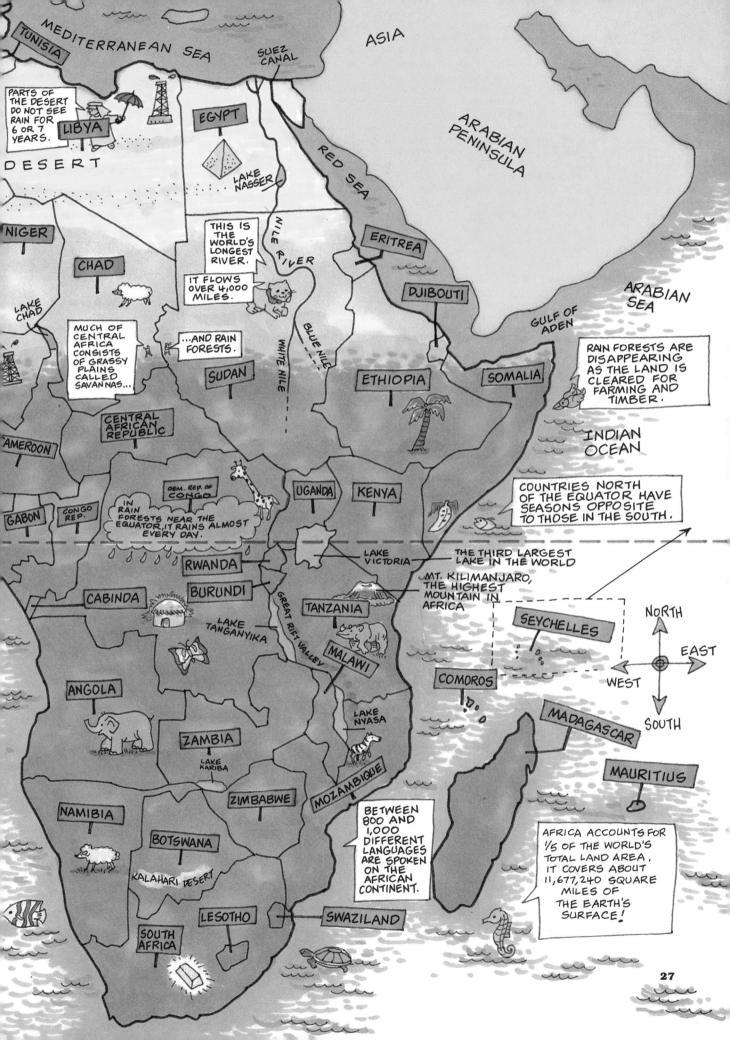

MEDITERRANEAN SEA

ASIA

TUNISIA

SUEZ CANAL

PARTS OF THE DESERT DO NOT SEE RAIN FOR 6 OR 7 YEARS.

LIBYA

EGYPT

LAKE NASSER

RED SEA

ARABIAN PENINSULA

DESERT

NIGER

CHAD

THIS IS THE WORLD'S LONGEST RIVER.

IT FLOWS OVER 4,000 MILES.

NILE RIVER

ERITREA

DJIBOUTI

GULF OF ADEN

ARABIAN SEA

LAKE CHAD

MUCH OF CENTRAL AFRICA CONSISTS OF GRASSY PLAINS CALLED SAVANNAS...

...AND RAIN FORESTS.

SUDAN

WHITE NILE

BLUE NILE

ETHIOPIA

SOMALIA

RAIN FORESTS ARE DISAPPEARING AS THE LAND IS CLEARED FOR FARMING AND TIMBER.

CAMEROON

CENTRAL AFRICAN REPUBLIC

INDIAN OCEAN

GABON

CONGO REP.

DEM. REP. OF CONGO

IN RAIN FORESTS NEAR THE EQUATOR, IT RAINS ALMOST EVERY DAY.

UGANDA

KENYA

COUNTRIES NORTH OF THE EQUATOR HAVE SEASONS OPPOSITE TO THOSE IN THE SOUTH.

RWANDA

LAKE VICTORIA

THE THIRD LARGEST LAKE IN THE WORLD

MT. KILIMANJARO, THE HIGHEST MOUNTAIN IN AFRICA

CABINDA

BURUNDI

GREAT RIFT VALLEY

TANZANIA

SEYCHELLES

NORTH

LAKE TANGANYIKA

MALAWI

COMOROS

EAST

WEST

ANGOLA

LAKE NYASA

MADAGASCAR

SOUTH

ZAMBIA

LAKE KARIBA

MAURITIUS

ZIMBABWE

MOZAMBIQUE

NAMIBIA

BETWEEN 800 AND 1,000 DIFFERENT LANGUAGES ARE SPOKEN ON THE AFRICAN CONTINENT.

BOTSWANA

KALAHARI DESERT

AFRICA ACCOUNTS FOR 1/5 OF THE WORLD'S TOTAL LAND AREA, IT COVERS ABOUT 11,677,240 SQUARE MILES OF THE EARTH'S SURFACE!

LESOTHO

SWAZILAND

SOUTH AFRICA

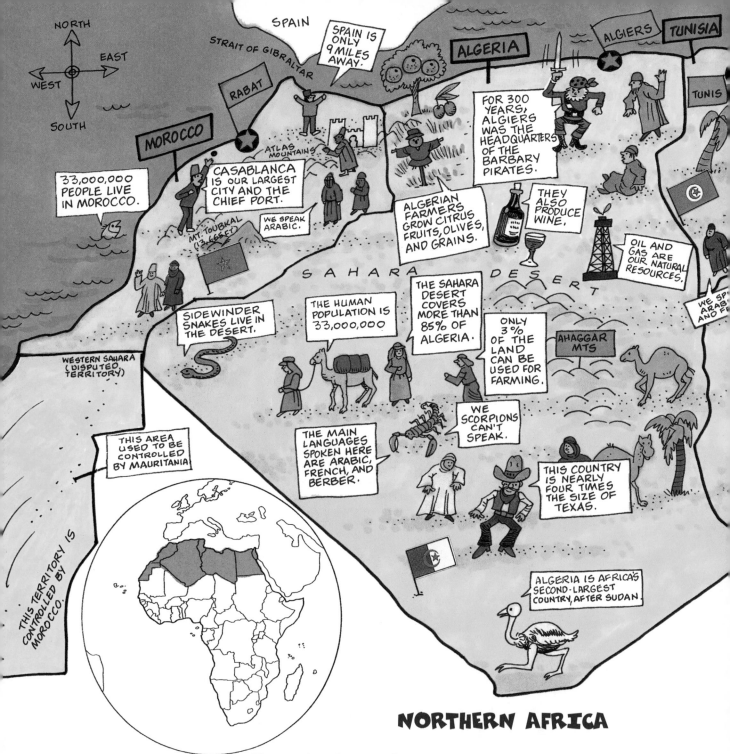

NORTHERN AFRICA

The peoples of ancient Greece, Rome, and Arabia influenced cultures in this part of Africa, and African culture—especially that of ancient Egypt—influenced them. In northern Africa today, Arabic is the dominant language and Islam is the major religion. Although Egypt is on the African continent, politically it often is considered part of the region known as the Middle East.

LEARN ABOUT NORTHERN AFRICA AS YOU LOOK FOR THESE FUN ITEMS:

- ❑ Barbary ape
- ❑ Beret
- ❑ Boats (3)
- ❑ Bunch of grapes
- ❑ Hyena

- ❑ Miner
- ❑ Mummy
- ❑ Orange tree
- ❑ Oil wells (4)
- ❑ Ostrich

- ❑ Palm trees (3)
- ❑ Pencil
- ❑ Pirate
- ❑ Pyramids (4)
- ❑ Scarecrow

- ❑ Scorpion
- ❑ Shovel
- ❑ Snake
- ❑ Thermometer

29

THE SAHEL

Just south of the Sahara Desert is a region called the Sahel, long inhabited by animal grazers and farmers. Much of the area is changing into desert as the Sahara expands southward at a rate of about three miles a year.

LEARN ABOUT THE SAHEL AS YOU LOOK FOR THESE FUN ITEMS:

- ☐ Anchor
- ☐ Basket
- ☐ Bird
- ☐ Camels (5)
- ☐ Cotton balls (3)
- ☐ Goat
- ☐ Elephant
- ☐ Fisherman
- ☐ Hippopotamus
- ☐ Lake Chad
- ☐ Niger River
- ☐ Peanuts (3)
- ☐ Periscope
- ☐ Soccer ball
- ☐ Sun
- ☐ Tent

THE HORN OF AFRICA

The region along Africa's northeastern coast is known as the Horn of Africa. On maps, its shape looks like the horn of a rhinoceros jutting into the Indian Ocean.

LEARN ABOUT THE HORN OF AFRICA AS YOU LOOK FOR THESE FUN ITEMS:

- ❏ Aardvark
- ❏ Acacia tree
- ❏ Banana
- ❏ Coffeepot
- ❏ Cotton
- ❏ Giraffes (2)
- ❏ Horseshoe

- ❏ Lion
- ❏ Marshmallow
- ❏ Nile crocodile
- ❏ Nubian Desert
- ❏ Oryx
- ❏ Ostrich
- ❏ Red Sea
- ❏ Umbrella
- ❏ White Nile
- ❏ Zebra

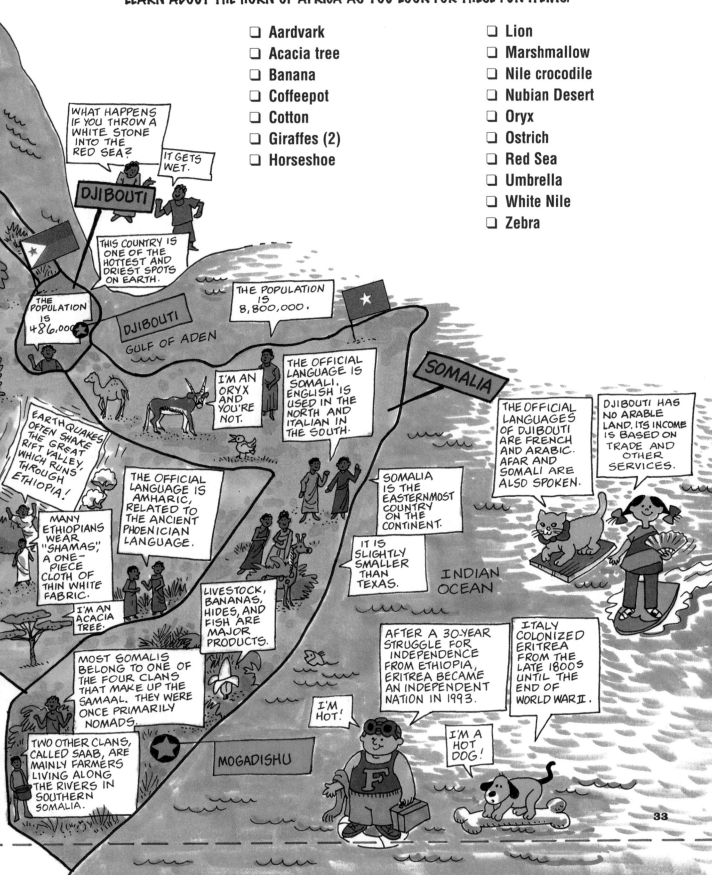

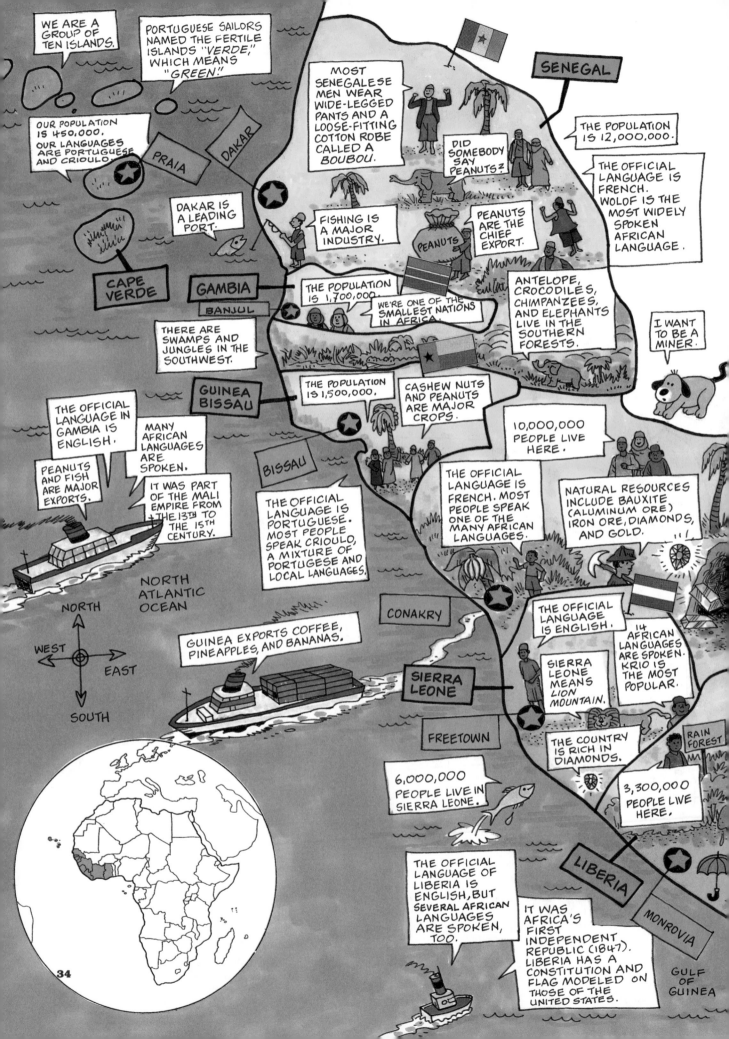

THE UPPER WEST COAST

Africa's upper west coast—the part that, seen on a map, bulges out into the Atlantic Ocean—has a landscape that varies from humid coastal plains and swamps to forested hills and plateaus. The soil is fertile, and farmers in this area grow such crops as cocoa, coffee, and peanuts.

During the era of the slave trade to the Americas, and for centuries before with other nations, coastal kingdoms of West Africa grew rich by trading slaves, gold, and ivory with Europeans.

LEARN ABOUT AFRICA'S UPPER WEST COAST AS YOU LOOK FOR THESE FUN ITEMS:

- ❑ Boats (4)
- ❑ Chocolate bar
- ❑ Coffeepot
- ❑ Crocodile
- ❑ Diamonds (4)
- ❑ Elephants
- ❑ Fishermen
- ❑ Game warden
- ❑ Gold bars (3)
- ❑ Lake Volta
- ❑ Lion
- ❑ Miner
- ❑ Pygmy hippopotamus
- ❑ Rain clouds (2)
- ❑ Umbrella

GUINEA

I'D LIKE A CHOCOLATE BAR.

I LOVE PEANUTS.

I SEE A CUTE LION.

CÔTE D'IVOIRE

GHANA

THE POPULATION IS 23,000,000.

THE OFFICIAL LANGUAGE IS ENGLISH, BUT THERE ARE MANY AFRICAN LANGUAGES SPOKEN HERE.

HISTORY IS RECITED BY STORY-TELLERS CALLED GRIOTS.

THE POPULATION IS 18,000,000.

THE OFFICIAL LANGUAGE IS FRENCH. AFRICAN LANGUAGES INCLUDE DIOULA, BAOULE, AND BETE.

BEFORE GAINING INDEPENDENCE FROM GREAT BRITAIN IN 1957, GHANA USED TO BE KNOWN AS THE GOLD COAST.

WE EXPORT COFFEE, COCOA, AND TROPICAL WOODS.

COCOA BEANS

YAMOUSSOUKRO

LAKE VOLTA

AN ENDANGERED SPECIES, THE PYGMY HIPPOPOTAMUS LIVES IN THE MARSHY SOUTHERN AREA OF GHANA.

THE COUNTRY WAS NAMED FOR THE IVORY TRADE, WHICH FLOURISHED FROM THE 13TH TO EARLY 20TH CENTURY.

RAIN FOREST

TODAY, IVORY TRADE IS ILLEGAL, AND THE NATION PROTECTS ITS ELEPHANTS IN GAME PRESERVES.

NATURAL RESOURCES INCLUDE GOLD, DIAMONDS, AND FISH.

ACCRA IS A MAJOR HUB FOR ROADS, RAILWAYS, AND SHIPPING.

WE EXPORT RUBBER, TIMBER, AND COCOA.

LIBERIA WAS FOUNDED FOR THE SETTLEMENT OF FREED AMERICAN SLAVES.

NO HUNTING

IT'S SAFE HERE.

CHOCOLATE

COCOA BEANS ARE THE NUMBER-ONE EXPORT.

ACCRA

35

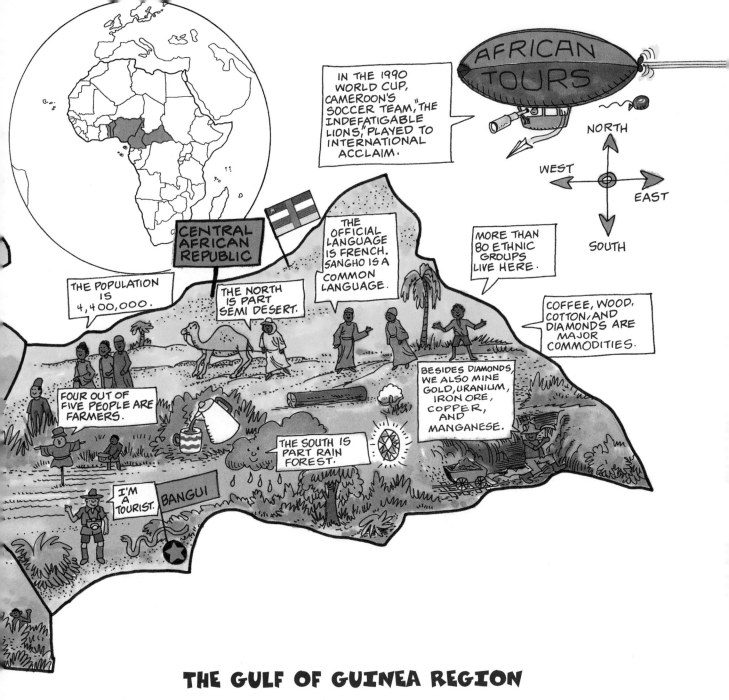

THE GULF OF GUINEA REGION

The Gulf of Guinea is a large section of the Atlantic that lies in the curve of Africa's bulging upper west coast. Many of the countries in this region share the "slave coast" history of the upper west coast countries (pp. 34-35). The gulf region has a richly varied landscape that includes old volcanic mountains, semidesert areas, swamps, tropical rain forests, and savannas. (*Savanna* is tropical or subtropical grassland.)

LEARN ABOUT AFRICA'S GULF OF GUINEA REGION AS YOU LOOK FOR THESE FUN ITEMS:

- ❏ Camera
- ❏ Cup
- ❏ Fishing poles (2)
- ❏ Giraffe
- ❏ Huts (2)
- ❏ Life preserver
- ❏ Oil wells (3)
- ❏ Paper airplane
- ❏ Red car
- ❏ Scarecrow
- ❏ Shark
- ❏ Snakes (2)
- ❏ Telescope
- ❏ Umbrellas
- ❏ Volcano

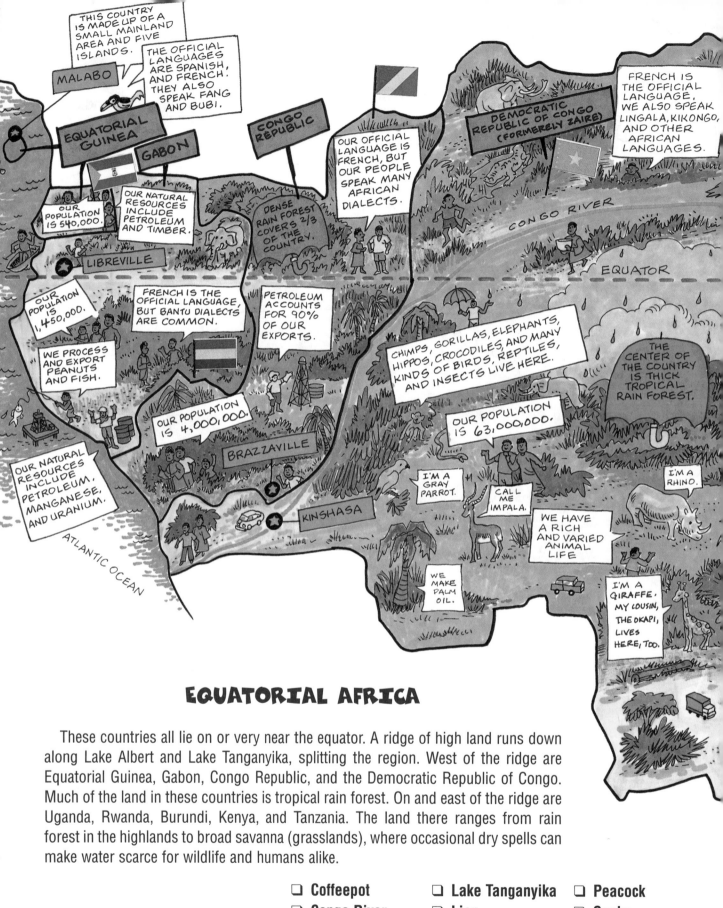

EQUATORIAL AFRICA

These countries all lie on or very near the equator. A ridge of high land runs down along Lake Albert and Lake Tanganyika, splitting the region. West of the ridge are Equatorial Guinea, Gabon, Congo Republic, and the Democratic Republic of Congo. Much of the land in these countries is tropical rain forest. On and east of the ridge are Uganda, Rwanda, Burundi, Kenya, and Tanzania. The land there ranges from rain forest in the highlands to broad savanna (grasslands), where occasional dry spells can make water scarce for wildlife and humans alike.

LEARN ABOUT EQUATORIAL AFRICA AS YOU LOOK FOR THESE FUN ITEMS:

- ❑ Coffeepot
- ❑ Congo River
- ❑ Crocodile
- ❑ Elephants (4)
- ❑ Gorilla
- ❑ Lake Tanganyika
- ❑ Lion
- ❑ Mount Kilimanjaro
- ❑ Parrot
- ❑ Peacock
- ❑ Snake
- ❑ Umbrellas (3)
- ❑ Zanzibar
- ❑ Zebra

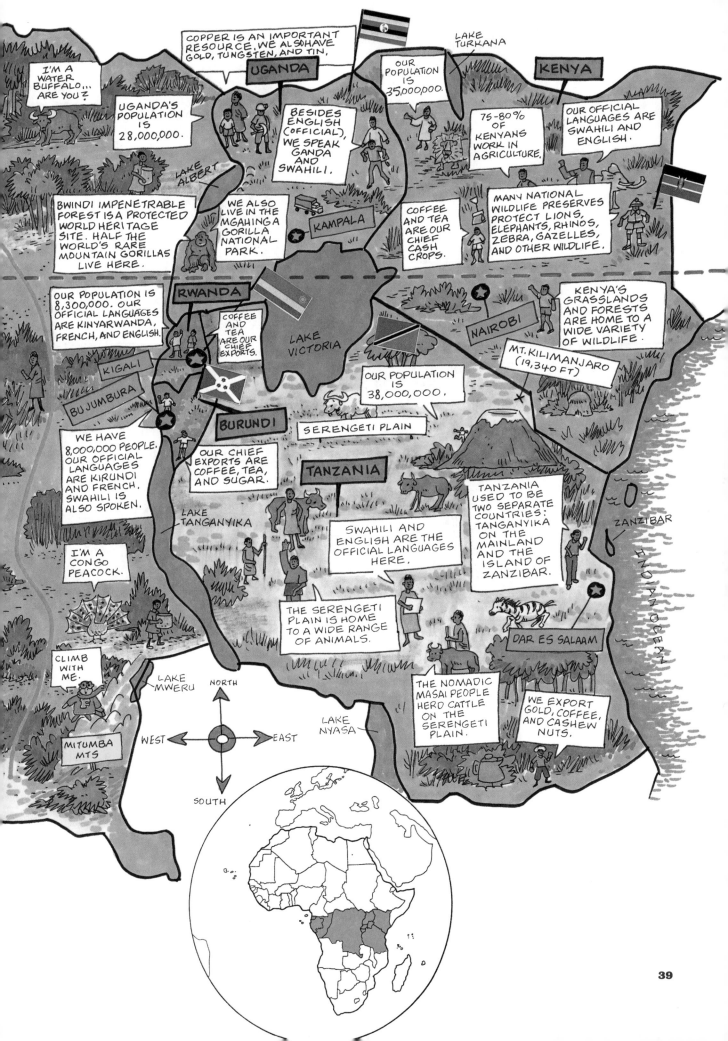

ANGOLA, ZAMBIA, MALAWI, AND MOZAMBIQUE

The region that lies south of the equatorial rain forests, between the South Atlantic Ocean and the Indian Ocean, has lots of open savanna and many farms. The area is home to antelope, elephants, giraffes, zebras, and many other animals.

LEARN ABOUT ANGOLA, ZAMBIA, MALAWI, AND MOZAMBIQUE AS YOU LOOK FOR THESE FUN ITEMS:

- ❑ Bananas (2)
- ❑ Cars (2)
- ❑ Coffee cups (2)
- ❑ Cow
- ❑ Eyeglasses
- ❑ Fish (3)

- ❑ Giraffe
- ❑ Hornbill
- ❑ Kariba Dam
- ❑ Leopard
- ❑ Rhinoceros
- ❑ Rice farmer

- ❑ Ring
- ❑ Scarecrow
- ❑ Shovel
- ❑ Snakes (2)
- ❑ Sun
- ❑ Victoria Falls

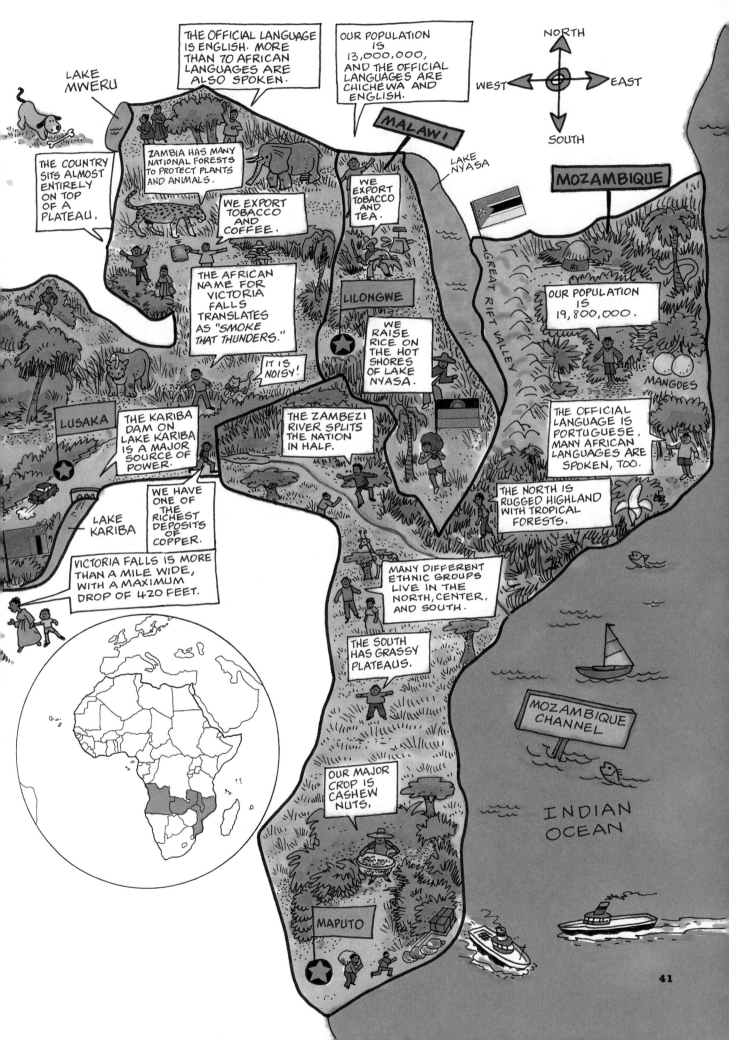

41

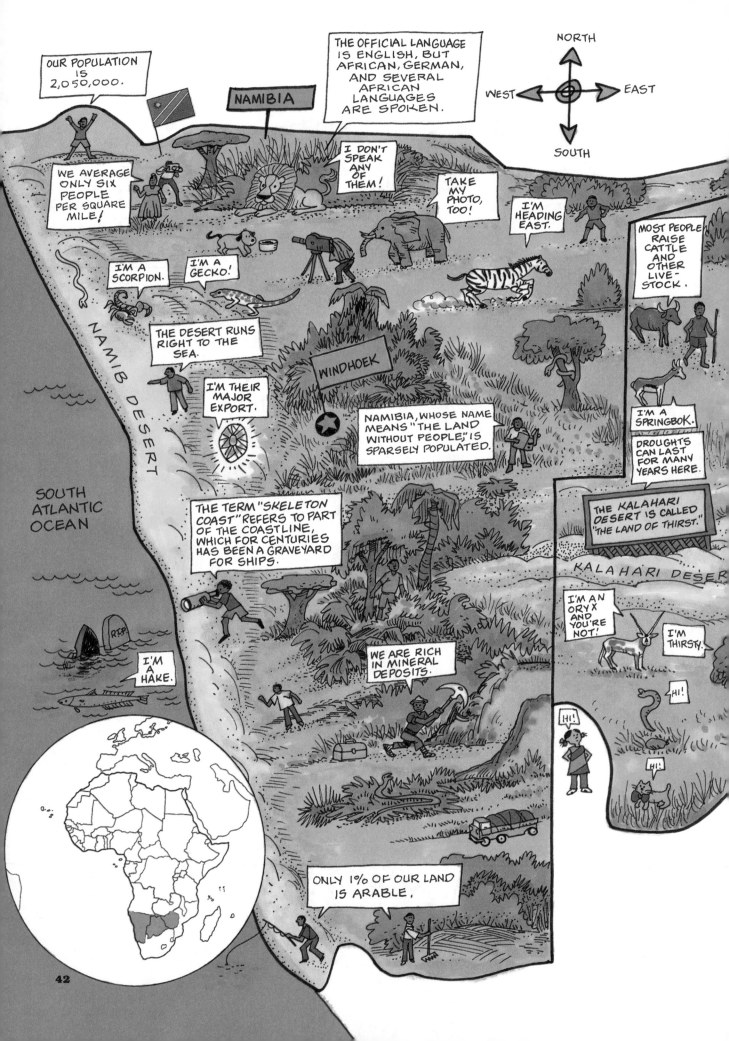

NAMIBIA, BOTSWANA, AND ZIMBABWE

Rich deposits of diamonds, gold, and minerals make this area one of the fastest-growing economic regions in Africa. Though rich in natural resources, such as diamonds and minerals, very little of the land in Namibia and Botswana is habitable. Namibia has only six people per square mile and Botswana has only seven. With its more-arable land and better-developed industries, Zimbabwe has 82 people per square mile.

LEARN ABOUT NAMIBIA, BOTSWANA, AND ZIMBABWE AS YOU LOOK FOR THESE FUN ITEMS:

- ❏ Baby
- ❏ Billboard
- ❏ Book
- ❏ Elephants (6)
- ❏ Fishing pole
- ❏ Lions (2)
- ❏ Lost snowman
- ❏ Namib Desert
- ❏ Oryx
- ❏ Picks (2)
- ❏ Rake
- ❏ Scorpion
- ❏ Shipwreck
- ❏ Snakes (5)
- ❏ Sneaker
- ❏ Snowman
- ❏ Truck
- ❏ Zebras (2)

SOUTH AFRICA, LESOTHO, AND SWAZILAND

The world's greatest diamond and gold mines are in South Africa, making it the richest country in Africa. The mines employ tens of thousands of men from neighboring countries.

Lesotho and Swaziland are two small, landlocked countries. One is completely surrounded by South Africa; the other is mostly so. Both are completely dependent on South Africa and Mozambique for trade routes to the ocean and other countries.

LEARN ABOUT SOUTH AFRICA, LESOTHO, AND SWAZILAND AS YOU LOOK FOR THESE FUN ITEMS:

- ❑ Cars (4)
- ❑ Citrus fruit
- ❑ Crown
- ❑ Drummer
- ❑ Giraffes (3)
- ❑ Grapes
- ❑ Guitar
- ❑ Lion
- ❑ Orange River
- ❑ Ostrich
- ❑ Pineapple
- ❑ Sailor
- ❑ Scarecrow
- ❑ Sheep (2)
- ❑ Shovel
- ❑ Table Mountain
- ❑ Tent
- ❑ Tractor
- ❑ Zebra
- ❑ Zulu warrior

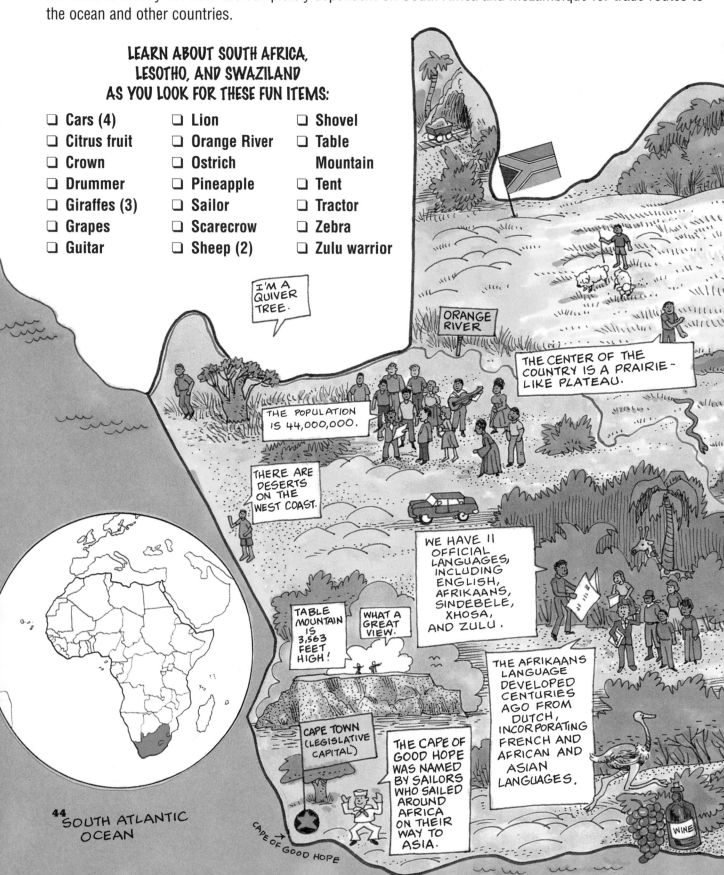

I'M A QUIVER TREE.

ORANGE RIVER

THE CENTER OF THE COUNTRY IS A PRAIRIE-LIKE PLATEAU.

THE POPULATION IS 44,000,000.

THERE ARE DESERTS ON THE WEST COAST.

WE HAVE 11 OFFICIAL LANGUAGES, INCLUDING ENGLISH, AFRIKAANS, SINDEBELE, XHOSA, AND ZULU.

TABLE MOUNTAIN IS 3,563 FEET HIGH!

WHAT A GREAT VIEW.

THE AFRIKAANS LANGUAGE DEVELOPED CENTURIES AGO FROM DUTCH, INCORPORATING FRENCH AND AFRICAN AND ASIAN LANGUAGES.

CAPE TOWN (LEGISLATIVE CAPITAL)

THE CAPE OF GOOD HOPE WAS NAMED BY SAILORS WHO SAILED AROUND AFRICA ON THEIR WAY TO ASIA.

CAPE OF GOOD HOPE

WINE

SOUTH ATLANTIC OCEAN

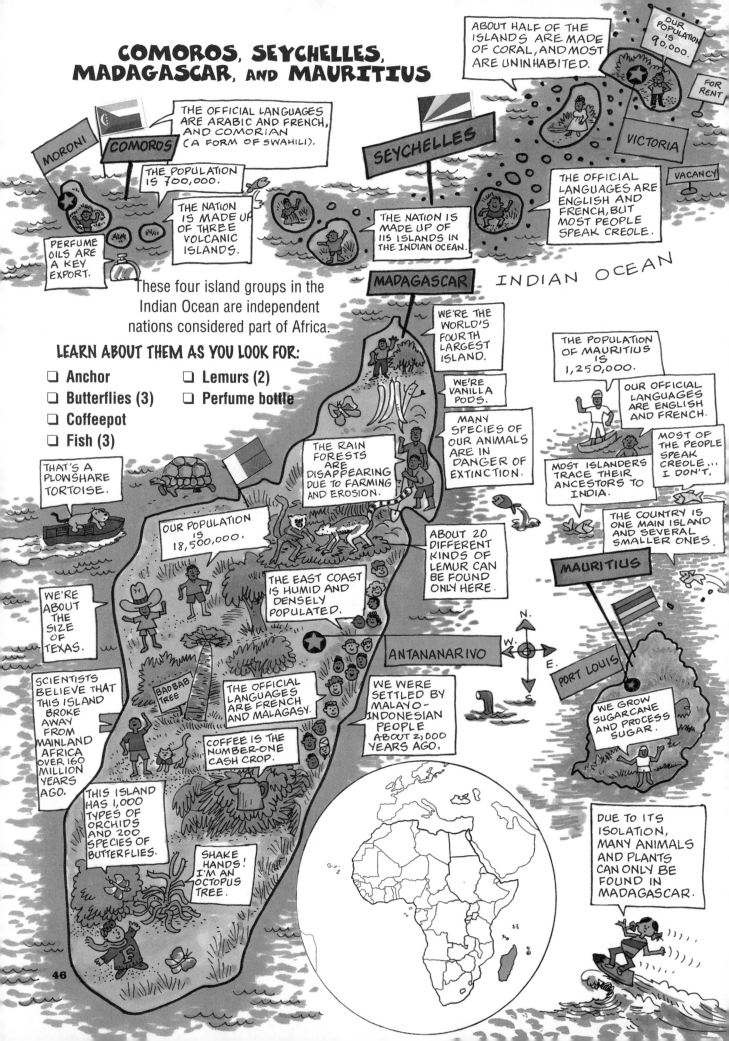

ANTARCTICA

With temperatures as low as -125° F, this continent is the coldest place on Earth. By international agreement, no one owns the land, and scientific research bases are the only inhabited places.

LEARN ABOUT ANTARCTICA AS YOU LOOK FOR THESE FUN ITEMS:

- ☐ Dinosaur
- ☐ Elephant seals (3)
- ☐ Lost mitten
- ☐ Snowman
- ☐ Snow- mobile

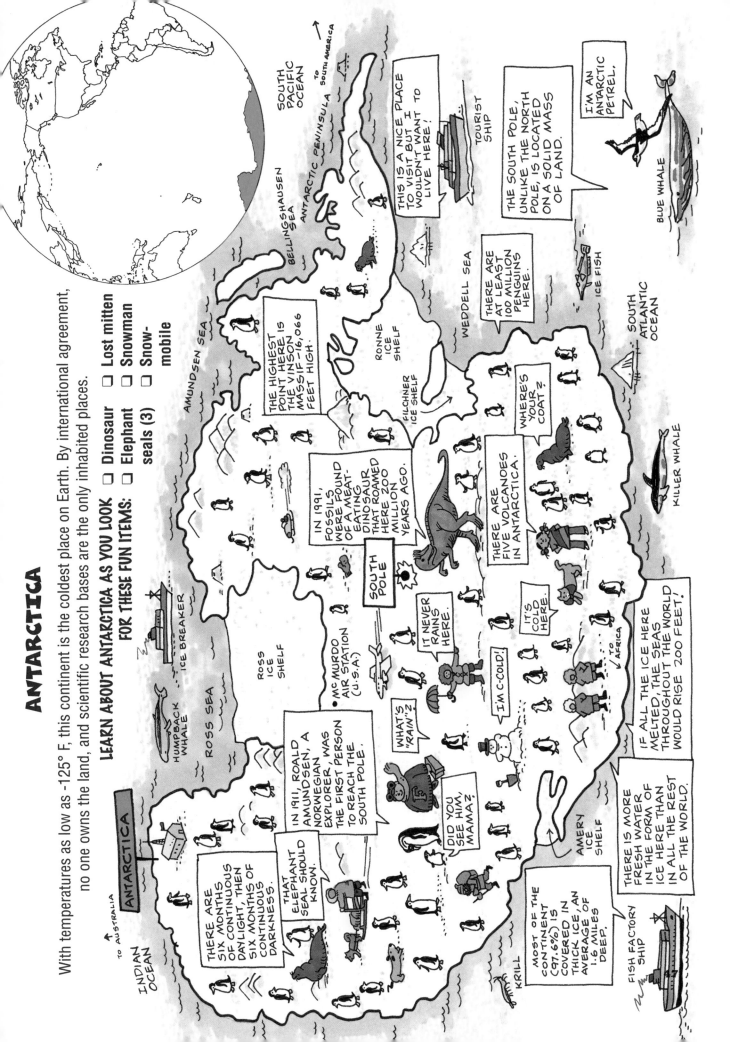

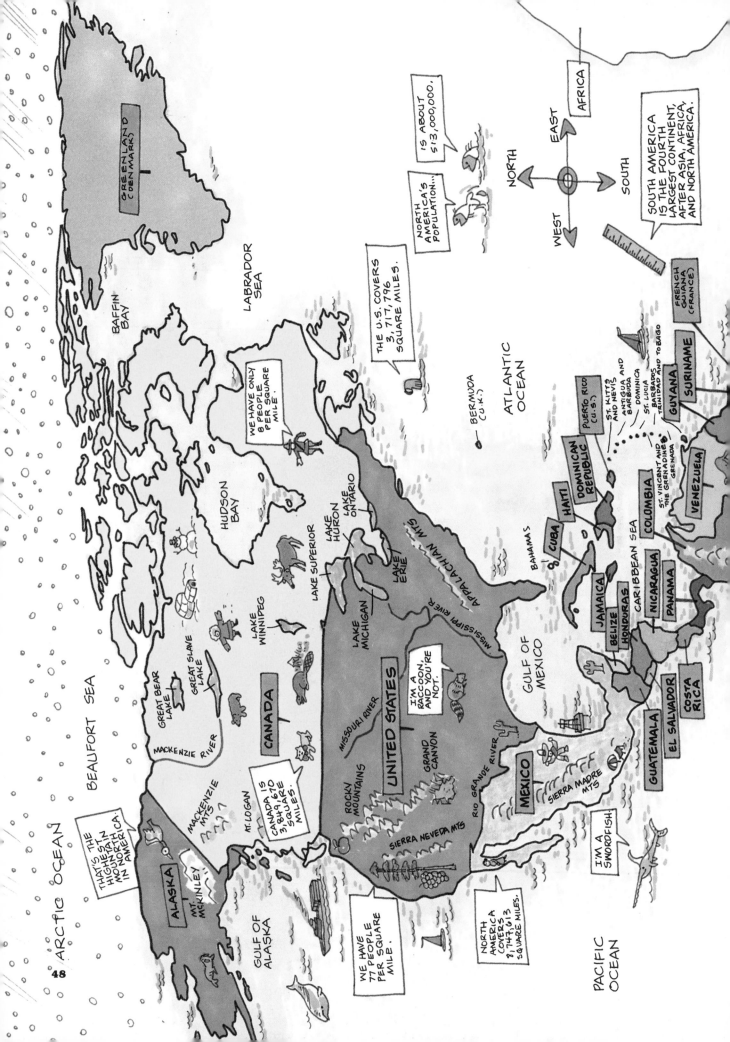

NORTH AMERICA AND SOUTH AMERICA

North America is the third largest of the seven continents. It stretches from Greenland and Canada in the Arctic north to Panama, which is near the equator. Islands in the Caribbean Sea are are also part of North America.

South America is the fourth largest continent. From equatorial Colombia, it extends farther south than any continent except Antarctica.

LEARN ABOUT NORTH AND SOUTH AMERICA AS YOU LOOK FOR THESE FUN ITEMS:

☐ Banana
☐ Cactuses (2)
☐ Coffeepot
☐ Igloo
☐ Monkey

☐ Moose
☐ Parrot
☐ Penguin
☐ Periscope
☐ Sailboats (2)

☐ Shipwreck
☐ Snowman
☐ Soccer player
☐ Surfer
☐ Swordfish

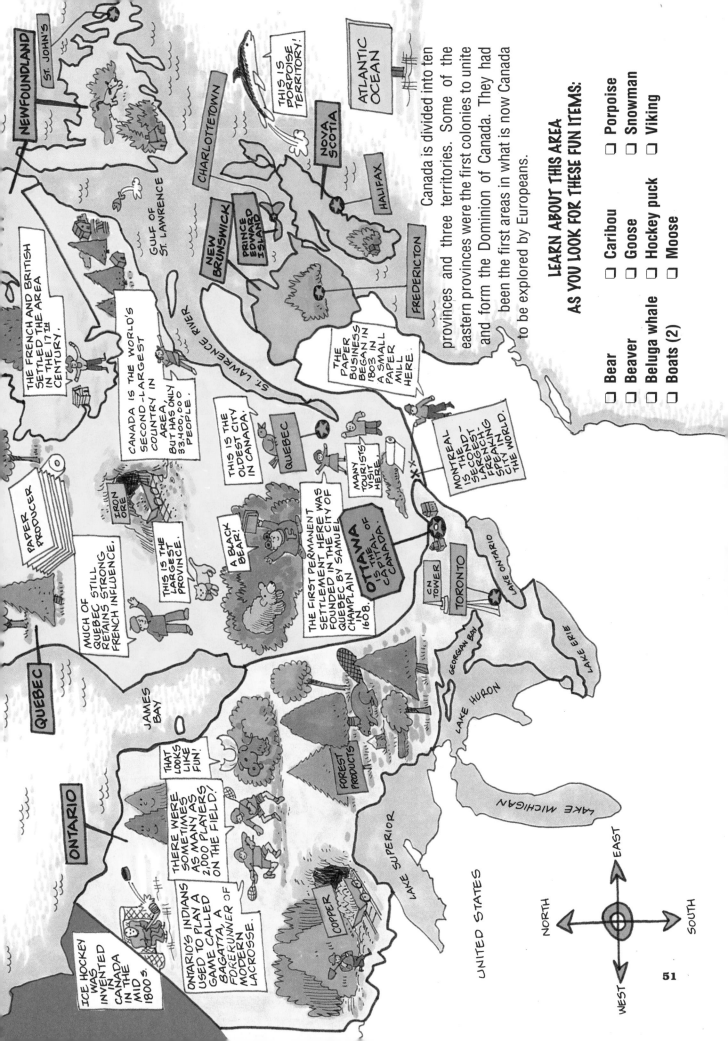

NEWFOUNDLAND

ST. JOHN'S

THIS IS PORPOISE TERRITORY!

CHARLOTTETOWN

ATLANTIC OCEAN

NOVA SCOTIA

HALIFAX

NEW BRUNSWICK

PRINCE EDWARD ISLAND

FREDERICTON

GULF OF ST. LAWRENCE

THE FRENCH AND BRITISH SETTLED THE AREA IN THE 17TH CENTURY.

CANADA IS THE WORLD'S SECOND-LARGEST COUNTRY IN AREA, BUT HAS ONLY 33,400,000 PEOPLE.

ST. LAWRENCE RIVER

THE PAPER BUSINESS BEGAN IN 1803 IN A SMALL PAPER MILL HERE.

THIS IS THE OLDEST CITY IN CANADA.

QUEBEC

MONTREAL IS THE SECOND-LARGEST FRENCH-SPEAKING CITY IN THE WORLD.

MANY TOURISTS VISIT HERE.

PAPER PRODUCER

IRON ORE

MUCH OF QUEBEC STILL RETAINS STRONG FRENCH INFLUENCE.

THIS IS THE LARGEST PROVINCE.

A BLACK BEAR!

THE FIRST PERMANENT SETTLEMENT HERE WAS FOUNDED IN THE CITY OF QUEBEC BY SAMUEL CHAMPLAIN IN 1608.

OTTAWA IS THE CAPITAL OF CANADA.

CN TOWER

TORONTO

LAKE ONTARIO

QUEBEC

JAMES BAY

ONTARIO

ICE HOCKEY WAS INVENTED IN CANADA IN THE MID 1800S.

ONTARIO'S INDIANS USED TO PLAY A GAME CALLED BAGATTA, A FORERUNNER OF MODERN LACROSSE.

THAT LOOKS LIKE FUN!

THERE WERE SOMETIMES AS MANY AS 2,000 PLAYERS ON THE FIELD!

FOREST PRODUCTS

COPPER

GEORGIAN BAY

LAKE HURON

LAKE ERIE

LAKE SUPERIOR

LAKE MICHIGAN

UNITED STATES

NORTH

EAST

SOUTH

WEST

51

Canada is divided into ten provinces and three territories. Some of the eastern provinces were the first colonies to unite and form the Dominion of Canada. They had been the first areas in what is now Canada to be explored by Europeans.

LEARN ABOUT THIS AREA
AS YOU LOOK FOR THESE FUN ITEMS:

- ☐ Bear
- ☐ Beaver
- ☐ Beluga whale
- ☐ Boats (2)
- ☐ Caribou
- ☐ Goose
- ☐ Hockey puck
- ☐ Moose
- ☐ Porpoise
- ☐ Snowman
- ☐ Viking

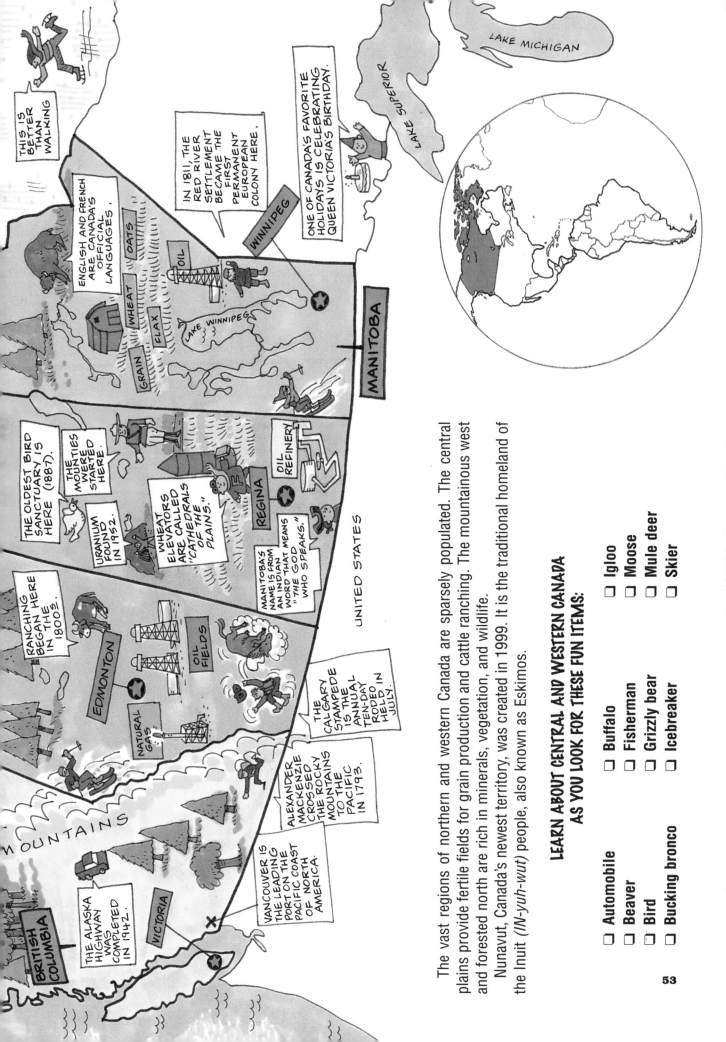

The vast regions of northern and western Canada are sparsely populated. The central plains provide fertile fields for grain production and cattle ranching. The mountainous west and forested north are rich in minerals, vegetation, and wildlife.

Nunavut, Canada's newest territory, was created in 1999. It is the traditional homeland of the Inuit (IN-yuh-wut) people, also known as Eskimos.

LEARN ABOUT CENTRAL AND WESTERN CANADA AS YOU LOOK FOR THESE FUN ITEMS:

- ☐ Automobile
- ☐ Beaver
- ☐ Bird
- ☐ Bucking bronco

- ☐ Buffalo
- ☐ Fisherman
- ☐ Grizzly bear
- ☐ Icebreaker

- ☐ Igloo
- ☐ Moose
- ☐ Mule deer
- ☐ Skier

THE UNITED STATES OF AMERICA

The United States of America is the world's third-largest country in population (after China and India) and the fourth-largest in land area (after Russia, China, and Canada). Its huge economic, political, and military influence make it the world's leading superpower.

In the 18th century, Britain ruled 13 American colonies. The U.S. became an independent nation in 1776, when it rebelled against British rule. Those colonies became the original 13 states. Today, the U.S. is a nation of 50 states. Washington, D.C., is the national capital and federal district. Outlying territories and other areas include Puerto Rico, the U.S. Virgin Islands, and Guam.

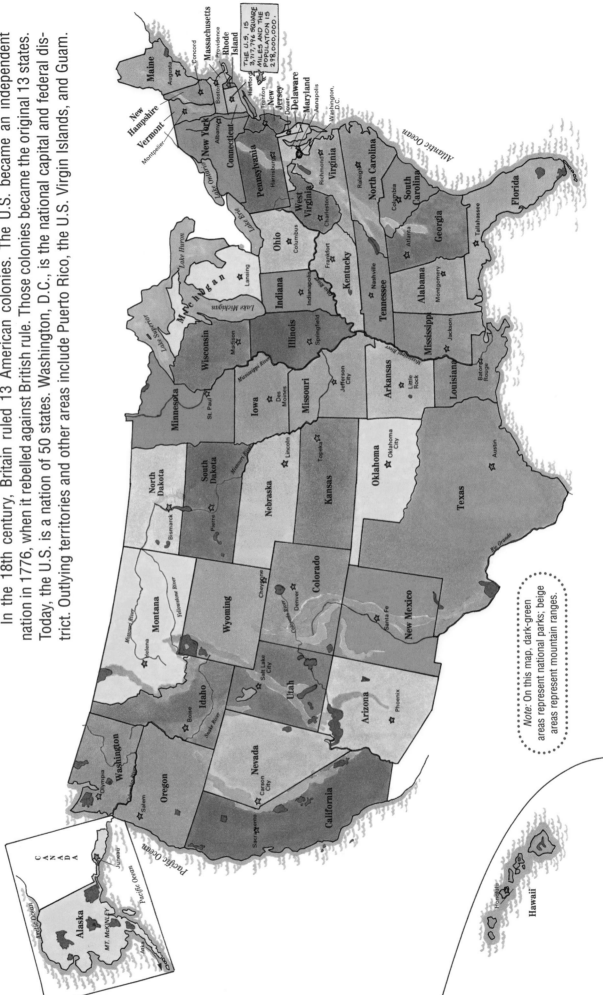

THE U.S. IS 3,717,796 SQUARE MILES AND THE POPULATION IS 298,000,000.

Note: On this map, dark-green areas represent national parks; beige areas represent mountain ranges.

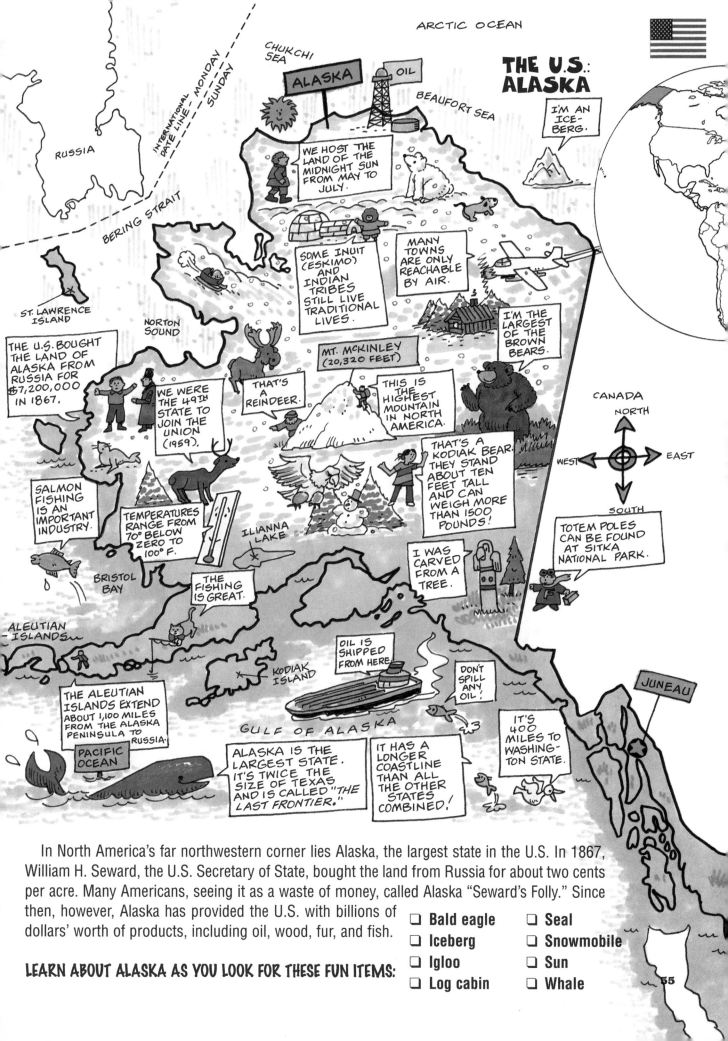

In North America's far northwestern corner lies Alaska, the largest state in the U.S. In 1867, William H. Seward, the U.S. Secretary of State, bought the land from Russia for about two cents per acre. Many Americans, seeing it as a waste of money, called Alaska "Seward's Folly." Since then, however, Alaska has provided the U.S. with billions of dollars' worth of products, including oil, wood, fur, and fish.

LEARN ABOUT ALASKA AS YOU LOOK FOR THESE FUN ITEMS:

- ❏ Bald eagle
- ❏ Iceberg
- ❏ Igloo
- ❏ Log cabin
- ❏ Seal
- ❏ Snowmobile
- ❏ Sun
- ❏ Whale

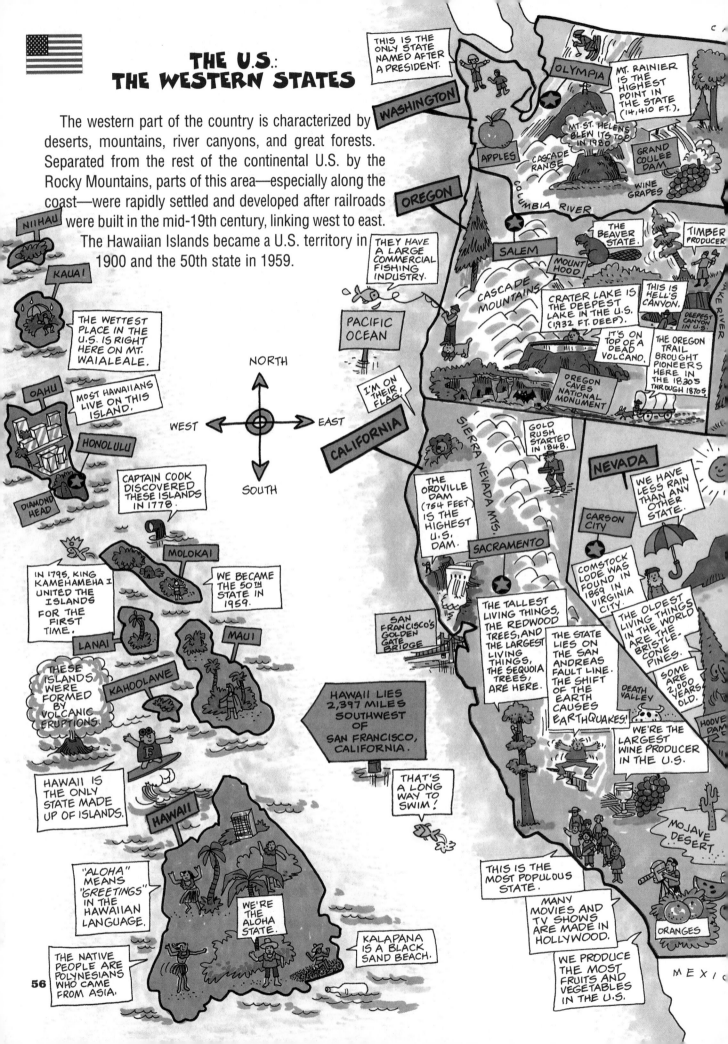

THE U.S.: THE WESTERN STATES

The western part of the country is characterized by deserts, mountains, river canyons, and great forests. Separated from the rest of the continental U.S. by the Rocky Mountains, parts of this area—especially along the coast—were rapidly settled and developed after railroads were built in the mid-19th century, linking west to east.

The Hawaiian Islands became a U.S. territory in 1900 and the 50th state in 1959.

THIS IS THE ONLY STATE NAMED AFTER A PRESIDENT.

WASHINGTON

OLYMPIA

MT. RAINIER IS THE HIGHEST POINT IN THE STATE (14,410 FT.).

MT. ST. HELENS BLEW ITS TOP IN 1980.

CASCADE RANGE

GRAND COULEE DAM

APPLES

WINE GRAPES

OREGON

COLUMBIA RIVER

THE BEAVER STATE.

TIMBER PRODUCER

SALEM

MOUNT HOOD

CASCADE MOUNTAINS

CRATER LAKE IS THE DEEPEST LAKE IN THE U.S. (1,932 FT. DEEP).

THIS IS HELL'S CANYON.

DEEPEST CANYON IN U.S.

THEY HAVE A LARGE COMMERCIAL FISHING INDUSTRY.

IT'S ON TOP OF A DEAD VOLCANO.

THE OREGON TRAIL BROUGHT PIONEERS HERE IN THE 1830S THROUGH 1870S.

PACIFIC OCEAN

OREGON CAVES NATIONAL MONUMENT

NIIHAU

KAUAI

THE WETTEST PLACE IN THE U.S. IS RIGHT HERE ON MT. WAIALEALE.

NORTH

I'M ON THEIR FLAG!

WEST — EAST

SOUTH

CALIFORNIA

SIERRA NEVADA MTS.

GOLD RUSH STARTED IN 1848.

NEVADA

WE HAVE LESS RAIN THAN ANY OTHER STATE.

OAHU

MOST HAWAIIANS LIVE ON THIS ISLAND.

THE OROVILLE DAM (754 FEET) IS THE HIGHEST U.S. DAM.

CARSON CITY

HONOLULU

CAPTAIN COOK DISCOVERED THESE ISLANDS IN 1778.

SACRAMENTO

COMSTOCK LODE WAS FOUND IN 1869 IN VIRGINIA CITY.

THE OLDEST LIVING THINGS IN THE WORLD ARE THE BRISTLE-CONE PINES.

DIAMOND HEAD

SOUTH

MOLOKAI

IN 1795, KING KAMEHAMEHA I UNITED THE ISLANDS FOR THE FIRST TIME.

WE BECAME THE 50TH STATE IN 1959.

THE TALLEST LIVING THINGS, THE REDWOOD TREES, AND THE LARGEST LIVING THINGS, THE SEQUOIA TREES, ARE HERE.

THE STATE LIES ON THE SAN ANDREAS FAULT LINE. THE SHIFT OF THE EARTH CAUSES EARTHQUAKES!

SOME ARE 2,000 YEARS OLD.

DEATH VALLEY

HOOVE DAM

LANAI

MAUI

SAN FRANCISCO'S GOLDEN GATE BRIDGE

THESE ISLANDS WERE FORMED BY VOLCANIC ERUPTIONS.

KAHOOLAWE

HAWAII LIES 2,397 MILES SOUTHWEST OF SAN FRANCISCO, CALIFORNIA.

WE'RE THE LARGEST WINE PRODUCER IN THE U.S.

HAWAII IS THE ONLY STATE MADE UP OF ISLANDS.

HAWAII

THAT'S A LONG WAY TO SWIM!

MOJAVE DESERT

"ALOHA" MEANS "GREETINGS" IN THE HAWAIIAN LANGUAGE.

WE'RE THE ALOHA STATE.

THIS IS THE MOST POPULOUS STATE.

MANY MOVIES AND TV SHOWS ARE MADE IN HOLLYWOOD.

ORANGES

THE NATIVE PEOPLE ARE POLYNESIANS WHO CAME FROM ASIA.

KALAPANA IS A BLACK SAND BEACH.

WE PRODUCE THE MOST FRUITS AND VEGETABLES IN THE U.S.

MEXICO

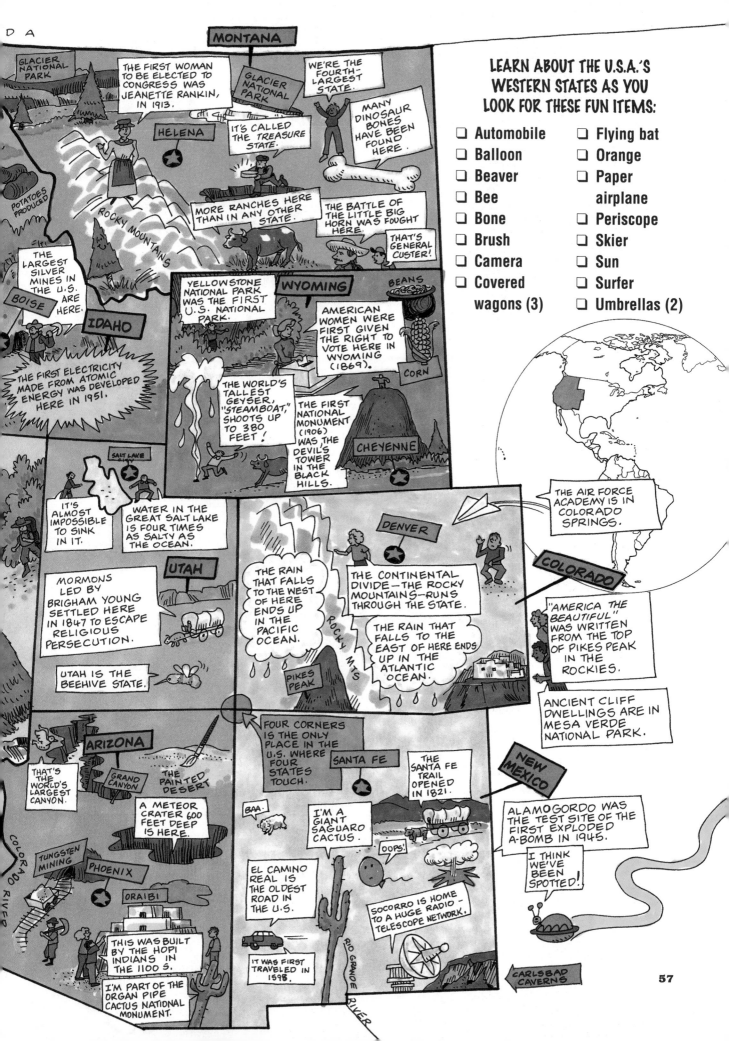

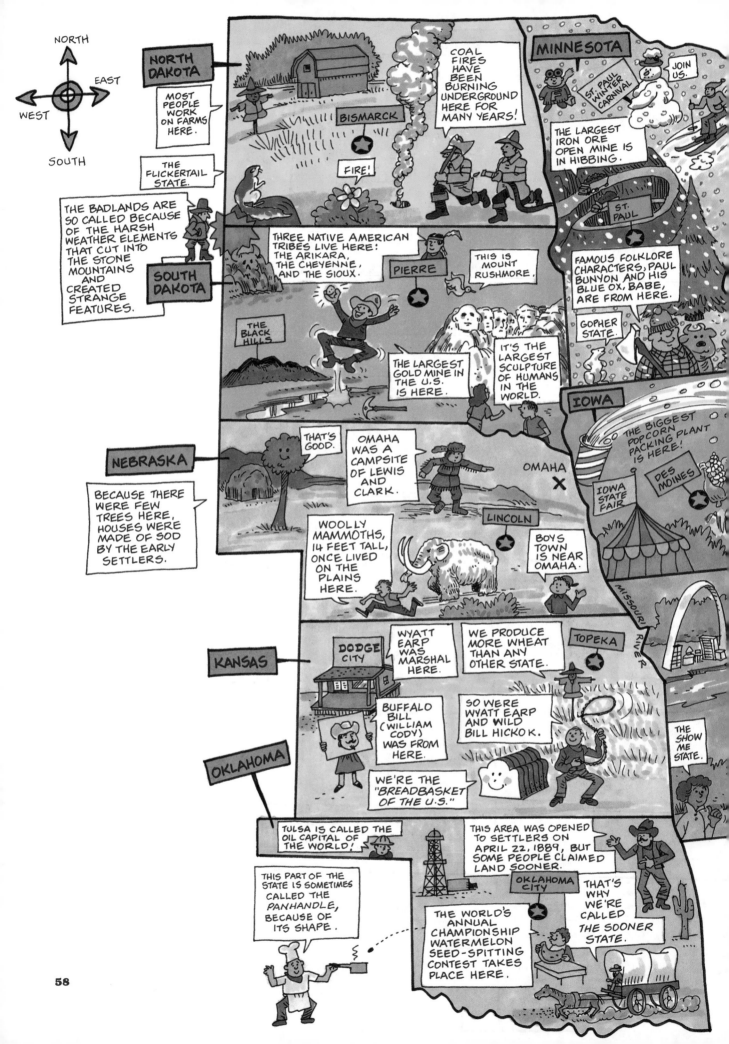

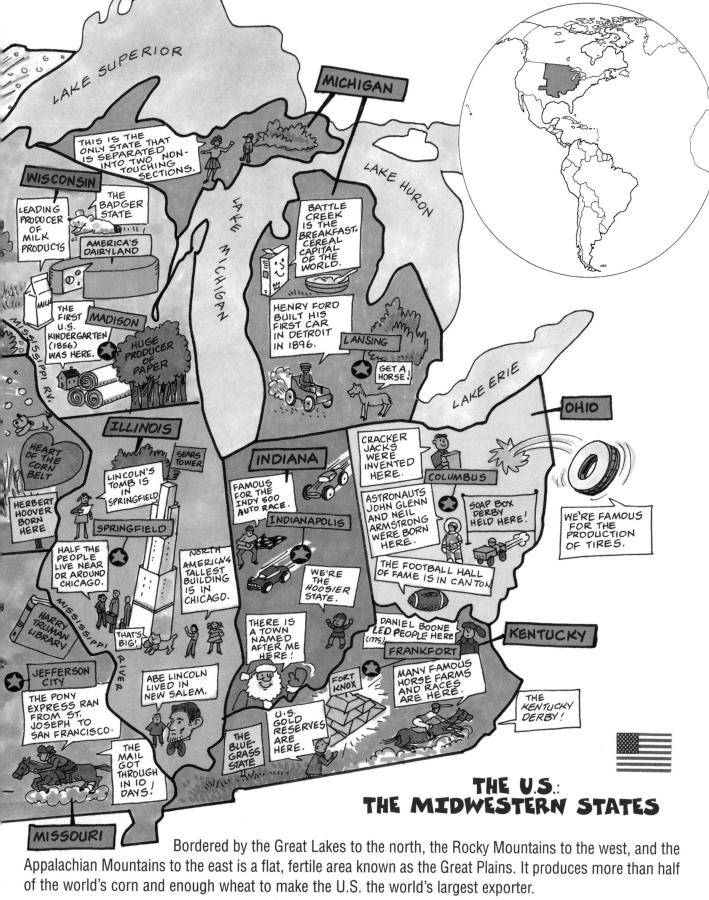

THE U.S.: THE MIDWESTERN STATES

Bordered by the Great Lakes to the north, the Rocky Mountains to the west, and the Appalachian Mountains to the east is a flat, fertile area known as the Great Plains. It produces more than half of the world's corn and enough wheat to make the U.S. the world's largest exporter.

LEARN ABOUT THE U.S.A.'S MIDWESTERN STATES AS YOU LOOK FOR THESE FUN ITEMS:

- ❑ Blue ox
- ❑ Book
- ❑ Cereal
- ❑ Flower
- ❑ Football
- ❑ Heart
- ❑ Race cars (3)
- ❑ Santa Claus
- ❑ Snowman
- ❑ Tire
- ❑ Watermelon slice
- ❑ Woolly mammoth

THE U.S.:
THE NORTHEASTERN AND MIDATLANTIC STATES

The most populous region in the country, the northeast and midatlantic states were the first to be settled by Europeans. Colonists arrived from England in 1620 and settled in New Plymouth, Massachusetts.

LEARN ABOUT U.S.A.'S NORTHEASTERN AND MIDATLANTIC STATES AS YOU LOOK FOR THESE FUN ITEMS:

- ❏ Anchor
- ❏ Apple
- ❏ Baseball
- ❏ Basketball
- ❏ Cannon
- ❏ Kite
- ❏ Lighthouse
- ❏ Lobster
- ❏ Ship
- ❏ Skier
- ❏ Treasure chest
- ❏ Truck
- ❏ Umbrella

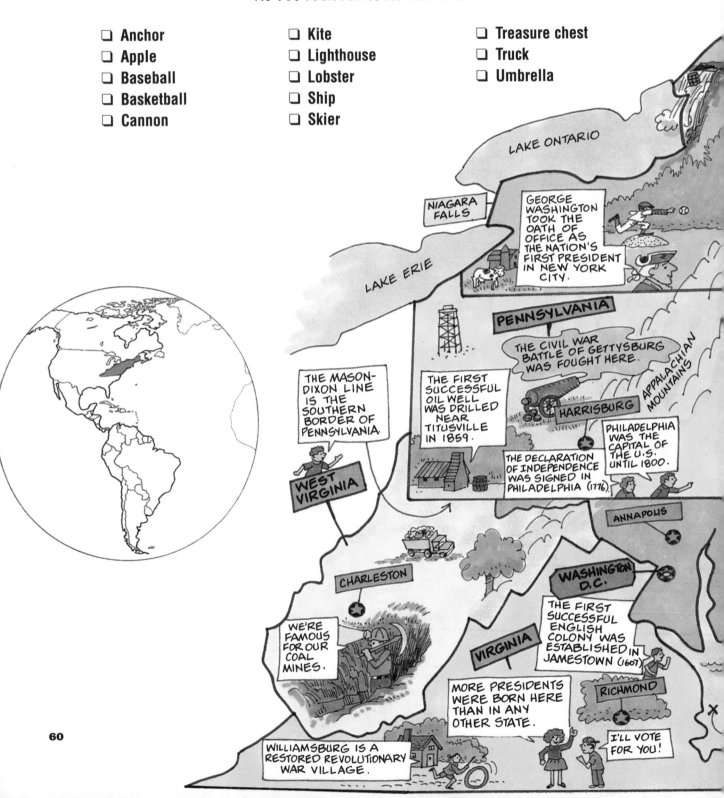

LAKE ONTARIO

NIAGARA FALLS

GEORGE WASHINGTON TOOK THE OATH OF OFFICE AS THE NATION'S FIRST PRESIDENT IN NEW YORK CITY.

LAKE ERIE

PENNSYLVANIA

THE CIVIL WAR BATTLE OF GETTYSBURG WAS FOUGHT HERE.

APPALACHIAN MOUNTAINS

THE MASON-DIXON LINE IS THE SOUTHERN BORDER OF PENNSYLVANIA.

THE FIRST SUCCESSFUL OIL WELL WAS DRILLED NEAR TITUSVILLE IN 1859.

HARRISBURG

PHILADELPHIA WAS THE CAPITAL OF THE U.S. UNTIL 1800.

THE DECLARATION OF INDEPENDENCE WAS SIGNED IN PHILADELPHIA (1776)

WEST VIRGINIA

ANNAPOLIS

CHARLESTON

WASHINGTON D.C.

WE'RE FAMOUS FOR OUR COAL MINES.

THE FIRST SUCCESSFUL ENGLISH COLONY WAS ESTABLISHED IN JAMESTOWN (1607)

VIRGINIA

MORE PRESIDENTS WERE BORN HERE THAN IN ANY OTHER STATE.

RICHMOND

I'LL VOTE FOR YOU!

WILLIAMSBURG IS A RESTORED REVOLUTIONARY WAR VILLAGE.

THE U.S.: THE SOUTHERN STATES

The southern states, which extend from the Atlantic coast to Texas, were once totally farm-based, producing mainly cotton and tobacco. Although still agricultural, the area is now strong in industry, and produces oil as well as iron and steel.

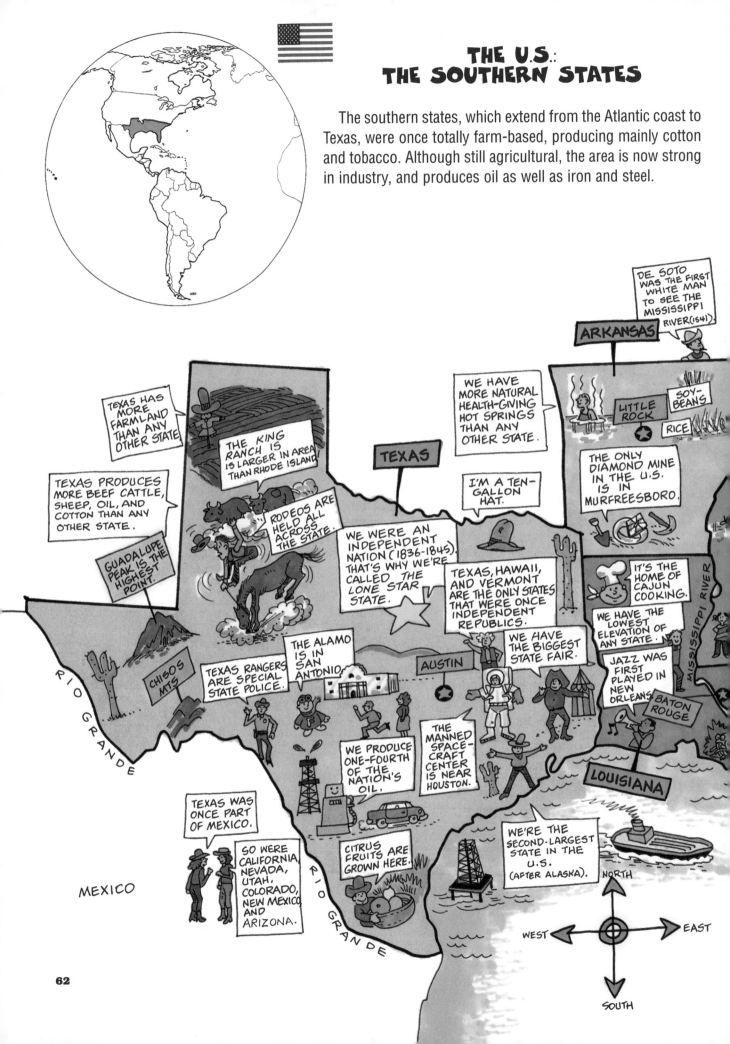

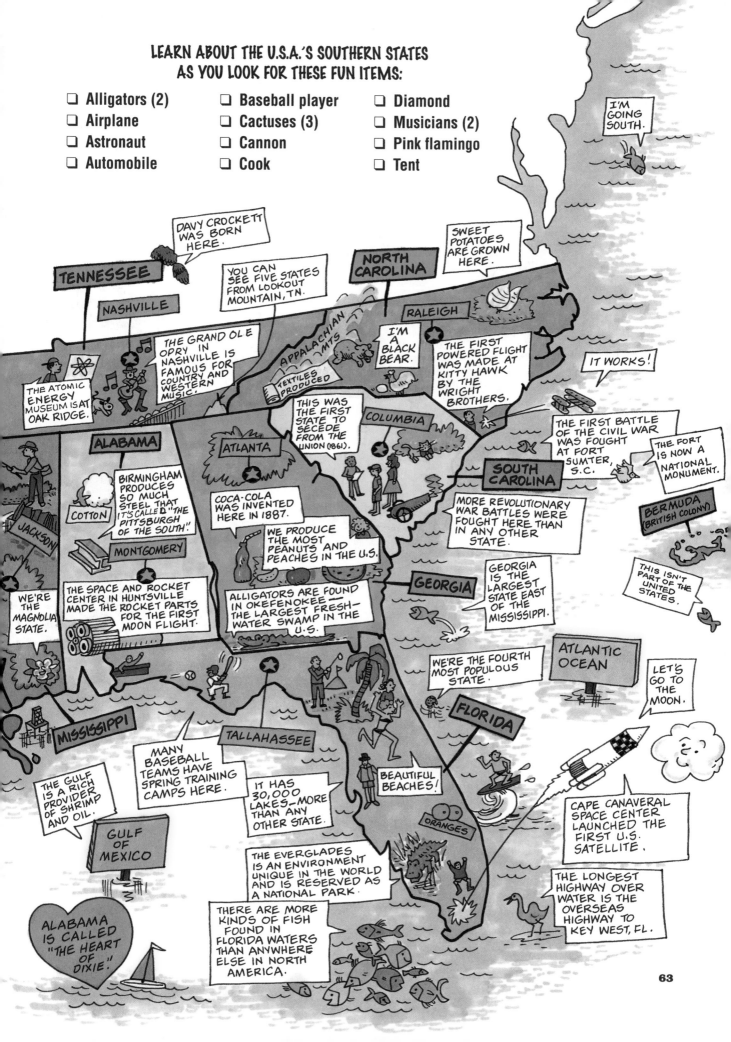

MEXICO AND CENTRAL AMERICA

The peoples of Mexico and Central America are mostly of Spanish or Indian ancestry, or a mixture of both. Mexico, a hot and dry region of North America, is rich in precious metals and petroleum. The seven countries of Central America are mainly agricultural. Dotted with active volcanoes, the land has jungles and high mountains, and the climate is hot and steamy, perfect for growing coffee, bananas, and other tropical crops.

LEARN ABOUT MEXICO, CENTRAL AMERICA, AND THE CARIBBEAN NATIONS AS YOU LOOK FOR THESE FUN ITEMS:

- ❏ Armadillo
- ❏ Coffeepots (3)
- ❏ Cotton (3)
- ❏ Diver
- ❏ Miner
- ❏ Oil well
- ❏ Photographer
- ❏ Pineapple
- ❏ Sailor
- ❏ Scarecrow
- ❏ Shovel
- ❏ Shrimp (3)
- ❏ Squash
- ❏ Turtle
- ❏ Umbrellas (3)

THE CARIBBEAN NATIONS

A chain of tropical islands about 2,000 miles long stretches across the Caribbean Sea, then curves like a hook toward South America. These islands were the first land in the Americas that Christopher Columbus saw and set foot on during his 1492 voyage of discovery. In the 16th century, Europeans colonized the islands, bringing African slaves to work plantations.

Today, 13 of the islands or island groups are independent nations (see list below). Others are territories of the U.S. or European countries. Most of the people living here are descendants of African slaves, Spanish conquerors, or both. Most countries in this region depend on tourism and agriculture for their income.

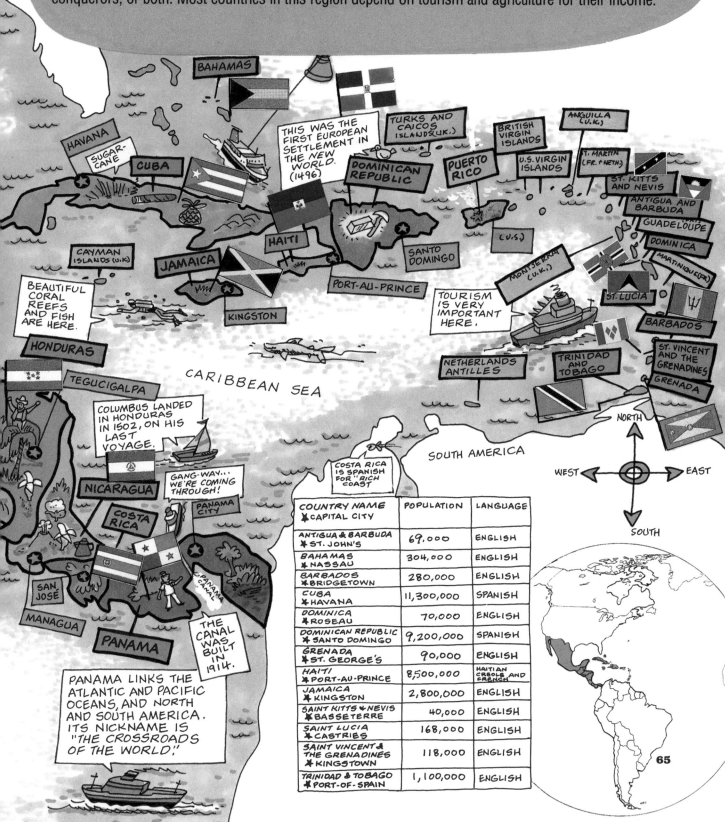

BAHAMAS

HAVANA

SUGAR-CANE

CUBA

THIS WAS THE FIRST EUROPEAN SETTLEMENT IN THE NEW WORLD. (1496)

TURKS AND CAICOS ISLANDS(U.K.)

DOMINICAN REPUBLIC

PUERTO RICO

BRITISH VIRGIN ISLANDS

U.S. VIRGIN ISLANDS

ANGUILLA (U.K.)

T. MARTIN (FR. + NETH.)

ST. KITTS AND NEVIS

ANTIGUA AND BARBUDA

GUADELOUPE

DOMINICA

MARTINIQUE(FR.)

CAYMAN ISLANDS (U.K.)

HAITI

JAMAICA

(U.S.)

SANTO DOMINGO

MONTSERRAT (U.K.)

ST. LUCIA

BEAUTIFUL CORAL REEFS AND FISH ARE HERE.

KINGSTON

PORT-AU-PRINCE

TOURISM IS VERY IMPORTANT HERE.

BARBADOS

HONDURAS

TEGUCIGALPA

CARIBBEAN SEA

NETHERLANDS ANTILLES

TRINIDAD AND TOBAGO

ST. VINCENT AND THE GRENADINES

GRENADA

SOUTH AMERICA

NORTH

WEST — EAST

SOUTH

COLUMBUS LANDED IN HONDURAS IN 1502, ON HIS LAST VOYAGE.

GANG-WAY... WE'RE COMING THROUGH!

NICARAGUA

COSTA RICA

PANAMA CITY

COSTA RICA IS SPANISH FOR "RICH COAST"

SAN JOSÉ

PANAMA CANAL

MANAGUA

PANAMA

THE CANAL WAS BUILT IN 1914.

PANAMA LINKS THE ATLANTIC AND PACIFIC OCEANS, AND NORTH AND SOUTH AMERICA. ITS NICKNAME IS "THE CROSSROADS OF THE WORLD."

COUNTRY NAME ✹CAPITAL CITY	POPULATION	LANGUAGE
ANTIGUA & BARBUDA ✹ST. JOHN'S	69,000	ENGLISH
BAHAMAS ✹NASSAU	304,000	ENGLISH
BARBADOS ✹BRIDGETOWN	280,000	ENGLISH
CUBA ✹HAVANA	11,300,000	SPANISH
DOMINICA ✹ROSEAU	70,000	ENGLISH
DOMINICAN REPUBLIC ✹SANTO DOMINGO	9,200,000	SPANISH
GRENADA ✹ST. GEORGE'S	90,000	ENGLISH
HAITI ✹PORT-AU-PRINCE	8,500,000	HAITIAN CREOLE AND FRENCH
JAMAICA ✹KINGSTON	2,800,000	ENGLISH
SAINT KITTS & NEVIS ✹BASSETERRE	40,000	ENGLISH
SAINT LUCIA ✹CASTRIES	168,000	ENGLISH
SAINT VINCENT & THE GRENADINES ✹KINGSTOWN	118,000	ENGLISH
TRINIDAD & TOBAGO ✹PORT-OF-SPAIN	1,100,000	ENGLISH

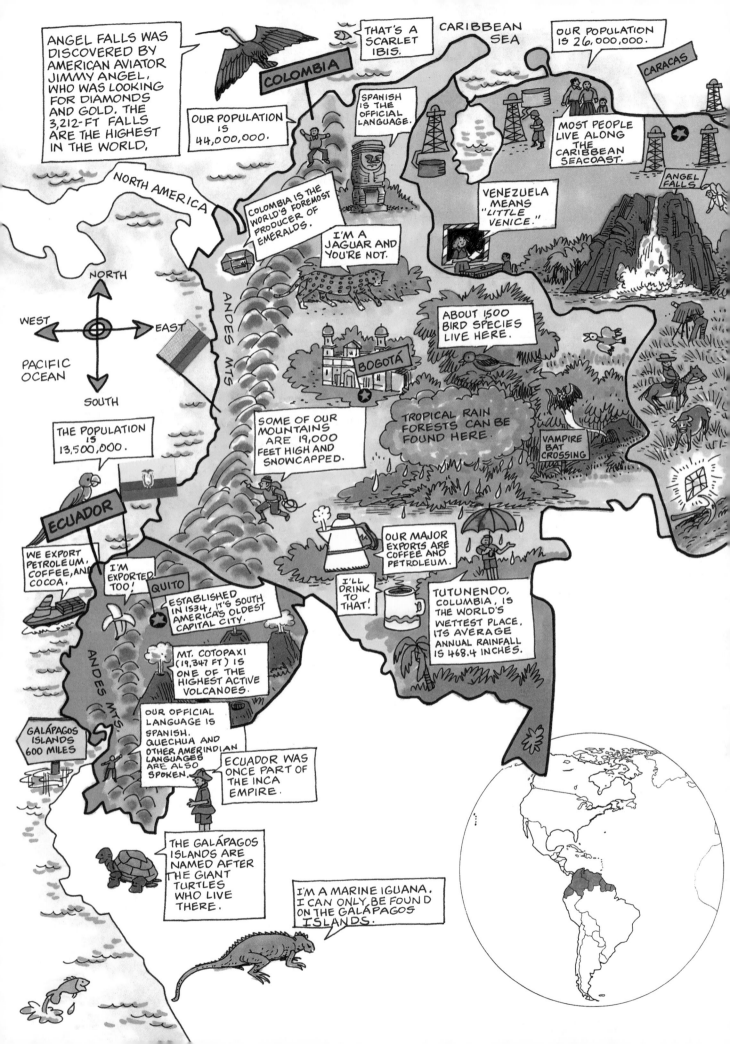

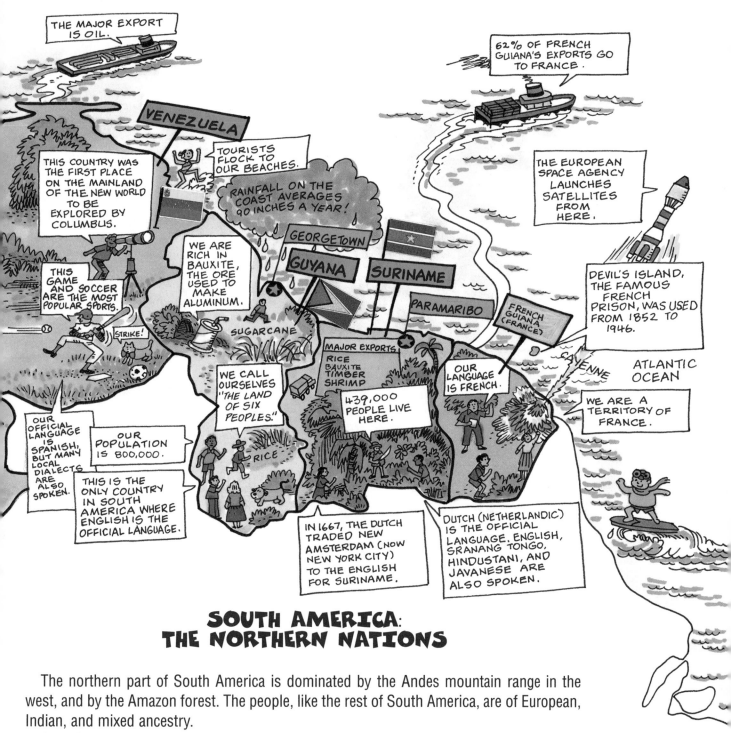

SOUTH AMERICA:
THE NORTHERN NATIONS

The northern part of South America is dominated by the Andes mountain range in the west, and by the Amazon forest. The people, like the rest of South America, are of European, Indian, and mixed ancestry.

Once Spanish colonies, Ecuador, Colombia, and Venezuela won their independence in the early decades of the 19th century. Guyana and Suriname gained their independence only recently: Guyana in 1966, from Britain; and Suriname in 1975, from the Netherlands. French Guiana is the only country on the South American mainland that is still a European territory.

LEARN ABOUT SOUTH AMERICA'S NORTHERN NATIONS
AS YOU LOOK FOR THESE FUN ITEMS:

- ❑ Aluminum can
- ❑ Angel
- ❑ Baseball bat
- ❑ Bat
- ❑ Cup
- ❑ Emerald
- ❑ Ibis
- ❑ Iguana
- ❑ Jaguar
- ❑ Mountain climber
- ❑ Photographer
- ❑ Satellite rocket
- ❑ Schoolteacher
- ❑ Soccer ball
- ❑ Stone idol
- ❑ Surfer
- ❑ Telescope
- ❑ Turtle

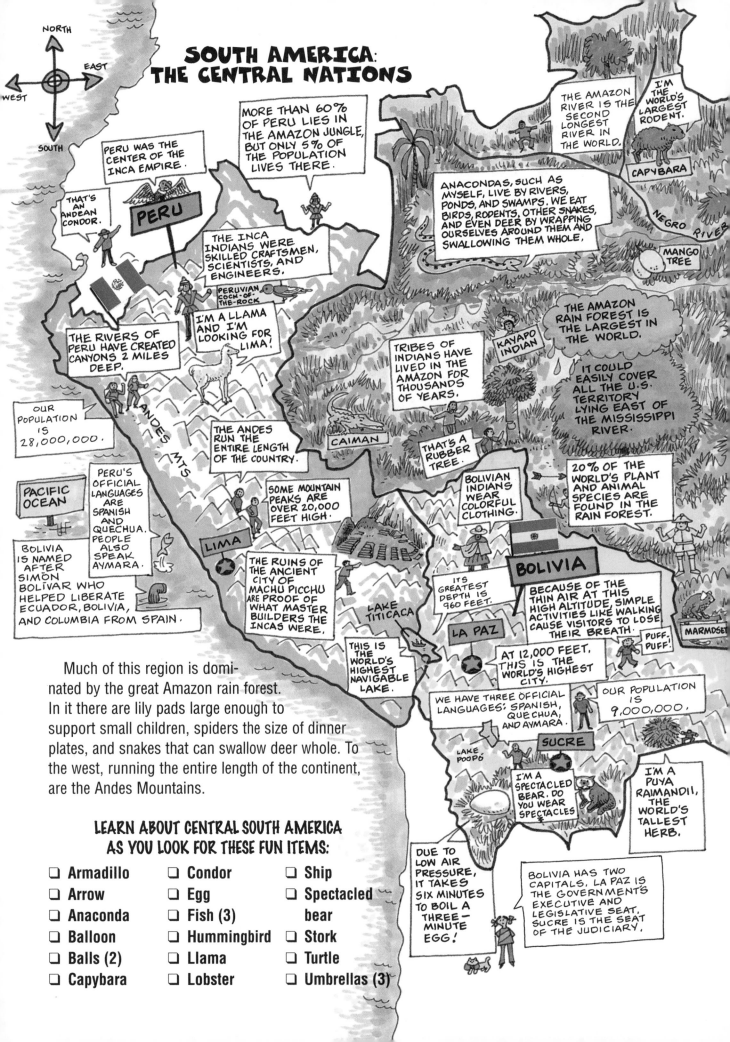

SOUTH AMERICA: THE CENTRAL NATIONS

NORTH
EAST
WEST
SOUTH

PERU WAS THE CENTER OF THE INCA EMPIRE.

THAT'S AN ANDEAN CONDOR.

MORE THAN 60% OF PERU LIES IN THE AMAZON JUNGLE, BUT ONLY 5% OF THE POPULATION LIVES THERE.

THE AMAZON RIVER IS THE SECOND LONGEST RIVER IN THE WORLD.

I'M THE WORLD'S LARGEST RODENT.

CAPYBARA

ANACONDAS, SUCH AS MYSELF, LIVE BY RIVERS, PONDS, AND SWAMPS. WE EAT BIRDS, RODENTS, OTHER SNAKES, AND EVEN DEER BY WRAPPING OURSELVES AROUND THEM AND SWALLOWING THEM WHOLE.

PERU

THE INCA INDIANS WERE SKILLED CRAFTSMEN, SCIENTISTS, AND ENGINEERS.

PERUVIAN COCK-OF-THE-ROCK

NEGRO RIVER

MANGO TREE

THE RIVERS OF PERU HAVE CREATED CANYONS 2 MILES DEEP.

I'M A LLAMA AND I'M LOOKING FOR LIMA!

TRIBES OF INDIANS HAVE LIVED IN THE AMAZON FOR THOUSANDS OF YEARS.

KAYAPO INDIAN

THE AMAZON RAIN FOREST IS THE LARGEST IN THE WORLD.

IT COULD EASILY COVER ALL THE U.S. TERRITORY LYING EAST OF THE MISSISSIPPI RIVER.

OUR POPULATION IS 28,000,000.

THE ANDES RUN THE ENTIRE LENGTH OF THE COUNTRY.

ANDES MTS

CAIMAN

THAT'S A RUBBER TREE.

20% OF THE WORLD'S PLANT AND ANIMAL SPECIES ARE FOUND IN THE RAIN FOREST.

PACIFIC OCEAN

PERU'S OFFICIAL LANGUAGES ARE SPANISH AND QUECHUA. PEOPLE ALSO SPEAK AYMARA.

SOME MOUNTAIN PEAKS ARE OVER 20,000 FEET HIGH.

BOLIVIAN INDIANS WEAR COLORFUL CLOTHING.

MARMOSET

BOLIVIA IS NAMED AFTER SIMON BOLIVAR WHO HELPED LIBERATE ECUADOR, BOLIVIA, AND COLUMBIA FROM SPAIN.

LIMA

THE RUINS OF THE ANCIENT CITY OF MACHU PICCHU ARE PROOF OF WHAT MASTER BUILDERS THE INCAS WERE.

BOLIVIA

BECAUSE OF THE THIN AIR AT THIS HIGH ALTITUDE, SIMPLE ACTIVITIES LIKE WALKING CAUSE VISITORS TO LOSE THEIR BREATH.

PUFF! PUFF!

LAKE TITICACA

ITS GREATEST DEPTH IS 960 FEET.

LA PAZ

AT 12,000 FEET, THIS IS THE WORLD'S HIGHEST CITY.

Much of this region is dominated by the great Amazon rain forest. In it there are lily pads large enough to support small children, spiders the size of dinner plates, and snakes that can swallow deer whole. To the west, running the entire length of the continent, are the Andes Mountains.

THIS IS THE WORLD'S HIGHEST NAVIGABLE LAKE.

WE HAVE THREE OFFICIAL LANGUAGES: SPANISH, QUECHUA, AND AYMARA.

OUR POPULATION IS 9,000,000.

SUCRE

LAKE POOPÓ

I'M A SPECTACLED BEAR. DO YOU WEAR SPECTACLES?

I'M A PUYA RAIMANDII, THE WORLD'S TALLEST HERB.

LEARN ABOUT CENTRAL SOUTH AMERICA AS YOU LOOK FOR THESE FUN ITEMS:

- ❏ Armadillo
- ❏ Arrow
- ❏ Anaconda
- ❏ Balloon
- ❏ Balls (2)
- ❏ Capybara
- ❏ Condor
- ❏ Egg
- ❏ Fish (3)
- ❏ Hummingbird
- ❏ Llama
- ❏ Lobster
- ❏ Ship
- ❏ Spectacled bear
- ❏ Stork
- ❏ Turtle
- ❏ Umbrellas (3)

DUE TO LOW AIR PRESSURE, IT TAKES SIX MINUTES TO BOIL A THREE-MINUTE EGG!

BOLIVIA HAS TWO CAPITALS. LA PAZ IS THE GOVERNMENT'S EXECUTIVE AND LEGISLATIVE SEAT. SUCRE IS THE SEAT OF THE JUDICIARY.

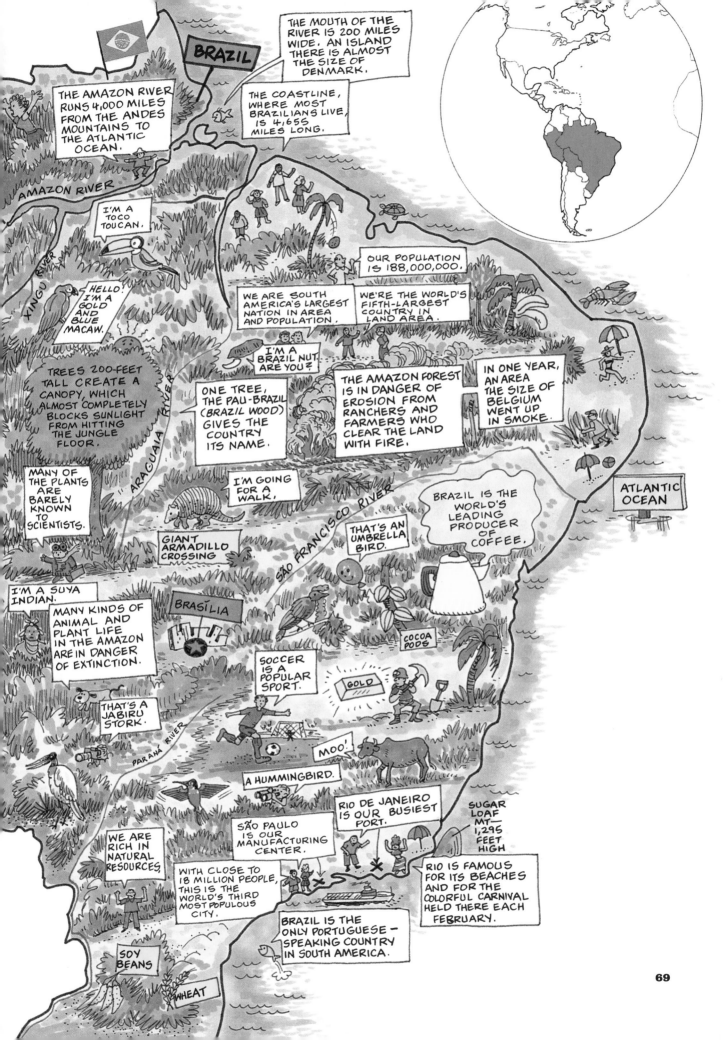

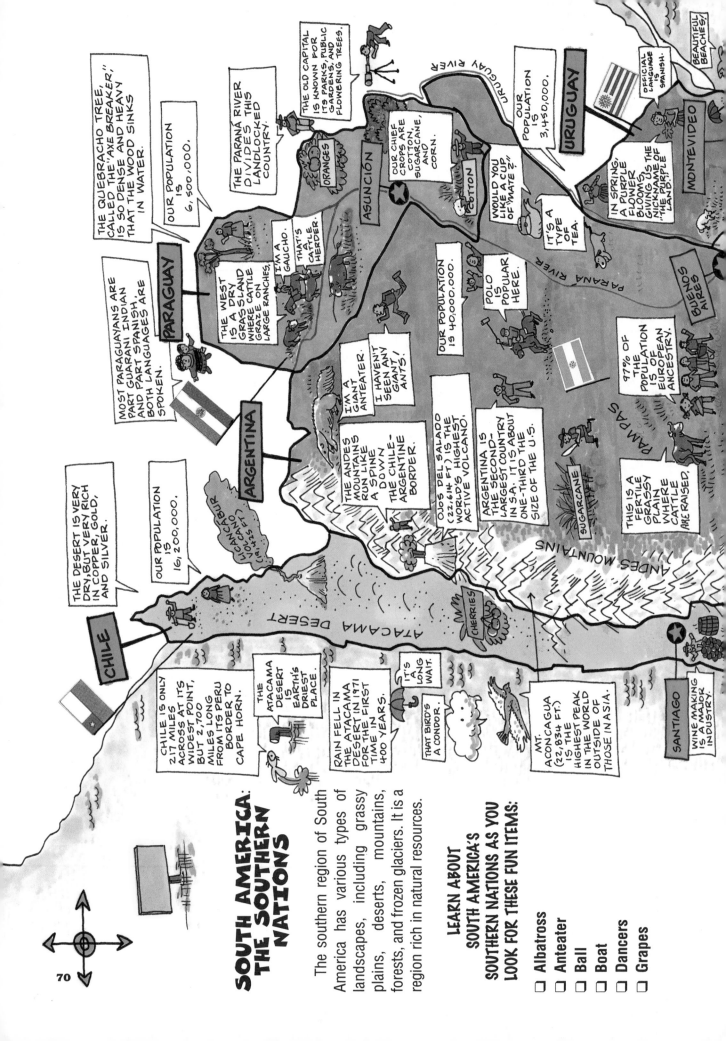

SOUTH AMERICA: THE SOUTHERN NATIONS

The southern region of South America has various types of landscapes, including grassy plains, deserts, mountains, forests, and frozen glaciers. It is a region rich in natural resources.

LEARN ABOUT SOUTH AMERICA'S SOUTHERN NATIONS AS YOU LOOK FOR THESE FUN ITEMS:

- ☐ Albatross
- ☐ Anteater
- ☐ Ball
- ☐ Boat
- ☐ Dancers
- ☐ Grapes

THE QUEBRACHO TREE, CALLED THE "AXE BREAKER," IS SO DENSE AND HEAVY THAT THE WOOD SINKS IN WATER.

OUR POPULATION IS 6,500,000.

THE PARANÁ RIVER DIVIDES THIS LANDLOCKED COUNTRY.

THE OLD CAPITAL IS KNOWN FOR ITS PARKS, PUBLIC GARDENS, AND FLOWERING TREES.

URUGUAY RIVER

OUR POPULATION IS 3,450,000.

OFFICIAL LANGUAGE IS SPANISH.

BEAUTIFUL BEACHES!

URUGUAY

MONTEVIDEO

IN SPRING, A PURPLE FLOWER BLOOMS, GIVING US THE NICKNAME OF "THE PURPLE LAND."

ORANGES

ASUNCIÓN

OUR CHIEF CROPS ARE COTTON, SUGARCANE, AND CORN.

COTTON

WOULD YOU LIKE A CUP OF MATE?

IT'S A TYPE OF TEA.

PARAGUAY

MOST PARAGUAYANS ARE PART GUARANÍ INDIAN AND PART SPANISH. BOTH LANGUAGES ARE SPOKEN.

THE WEST IS A DRY GRASSLAND WHERE CATTLE GRAZE ON LARGE RANCHES.

THAT'S A CATTLE HERDER.

I'M A GAUCHO.

OUR POPULATION IS 40,000,000.

POLO IS POPULAR HERE.

PARANÁ RIVER

BUENOS AIRES

97% OF THE POPULATION IS OF EUROPEAN ANCESTRY.

ARGENTINA

I'M A GIANT ANTEATER.

I HAVEN'T SEEN ANY GIANT ANTS!

THE ANDES MOUNTAINS RUN LIKE A SPINE DOWN THE CHILE-ARGENTINE BORDER.

OJOS DEL SALADO (22,614 FT.) IS THE WORLD'S HIGHEST ACTIVE VOLCANO.

ARGENTINA IS THE SECOND-LARGEST COUNTRY IN S.A. IT IS ABOUT ONE-THIRD THE SIZE OF THE U.S.

SUGARCANE

PAMPAS

THIS IS A FERTILE GRASSY PLAIN WHERE CATTLE ARE RAISED.

ANDES MOUNTAINS

THE DESERT IS VERY DRY, BUT VERY RICH IN COPPER, GOLD, AND SILVER.

OUR POPULATION IS 16,200,000.

LICANCÁBUR VOLCANO (19,425 FT.)

CHILE

CHILE IS ONLY 217 MILES ACROSS AT ITS WIDEST POINT, BUT 2,700 MILES LONG FROM ITS PERU BORDER TO CAPE HORN.

THE ATACAMA DESERT IS EARTH'S DRIEST PLACE.

ATACAMA DESERT

RAIN FELL IN THE ATACAMA DESERT IN 1971 FOR THE FIRST TIME IN 400 YEARS.

IT'S A LONG WAIT.

THAT BIRD'S A CONDOR.

CHERRIES

MT. ACONCAGUA (22,834 FT.) IS THE HIGHEST PEAK IN THE WORLD OUTSIDE OF THOSE IN ASIA.

SANTIAGO

WINE MAKING IS A MAJOR INDUSTRY.

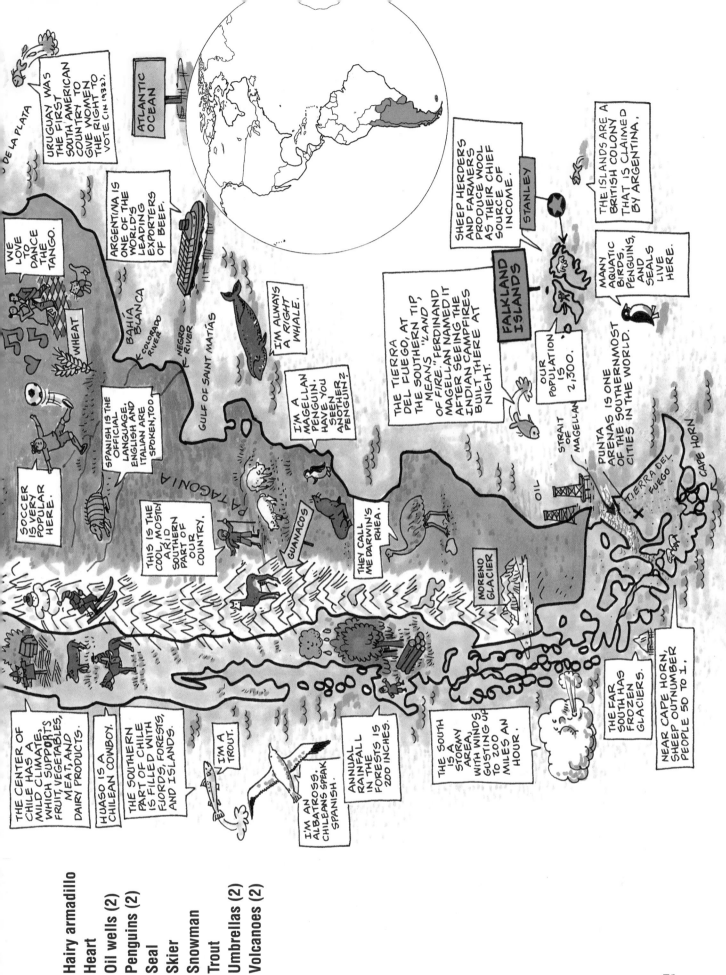

EUROPE

The seat of Western civilization, Europe has had a strong influence on the world through trade, exploration, and industry.

The continent stretches from the icy Arctic Circle in the north to the warm Mediterranean Sea in the south. Its western border is the North Atlantic Ocean and its eastern borders are the Ural and Caucasus mountains. The land—with its fertile plains and tall mountains—is as varied as its countries, peoples, and cultures.

LEARN ABOUT EUROPE AS YOU LOOK FOR THESE FUN ITEMS:

- ☐ Cyclist
- ☐ Eiffel Tower
- ☐ Fish (3)
- ☐ Grapes
- ☐ Puffin
- ☐ Sailboat
- ☐ Volcano
- ☐ Windmill
- ☐ Wooden shoe

FINLAND

RUSSIA

LAKE LADOGA

ESTONIA

LATVIA

LITHUANIA

BELARUS

FLAX

SUGAR BEETS

UKRAINE

MOLDOVA

WHEAT

DNIEPER RV.

DON RIVER

VOLGA RIVER

THE VOLGA (RUNNING FOR 2,290 MILES) IS THE LONGEST RIVER IN EUROPE.

EUROPE IS CONSIDERED THE BIRTHPLACE OF WESTERN CIVILIZATION.

CASPIAN SEA

ROMANIA

TRANSYLVANIAN ALPS

THE DANUBE RIVER FLOWS THROUGH 7 EUROPEAN COUNTRIES.

CAUCASUS MTS

THE HIGHEST POINT IN EUROPE IS MT. ELBRUS IN THE CAUCASUS RANGE IN RUSSIA.

THE BLACK SEA

NORTH

WEST

EAST

SOUTH

BULGARIA

TURKEY

AEGEAN SEA

EUROPE IS THE WORLD'S SECOND SMALLEST CONTINENT (ONLY AUSTRALIA IS SMALLER). YET IT RANKS THIRD IN POPULATION, AFTER ASIA AND AFRICA.

EUROPE HAS AN AREA OF ABOUT 4,000,000 SQUARE MILES.

ITS POPULATION IS 728,000,000.

THE LARGEST LAKE IN EUROPE IS LADOGA, IN RUSSIA (7,000 SQ. MILES).

UNITED KINGDOM AND IRELAND

The United Kingdom is a country made up of four parts: England, Wales, Scotland, and Northern Ireland. (The first three are also known as Britain.) Northern Ireland is on the same large island as the independent country of Ireland. In the late 19th and early 20th centuries, Great Britain was the world's leading industrial and trading nation. Its worldwide empire included Canada, India, Australia, New Zealand, and parts of Africa.

LEARN ABOUT THE UNITED KINGDOM AND IRELAND AS YOU LOOK FOR THESE FUN ITEMS:

- ☐ Bagpipe
- ☐ Big Ben
- ☐ Bus
- ☐ Deer
- ☐ Ferry
- ☐ Four-leaf clover
- ☐ Golf
- ☐ Knight in armor
- ☐ Lobster
- ☐ "Nessie"
- ☐ Sheep (3)
- ☐ Soccer ball
- ☐ Tennis racket

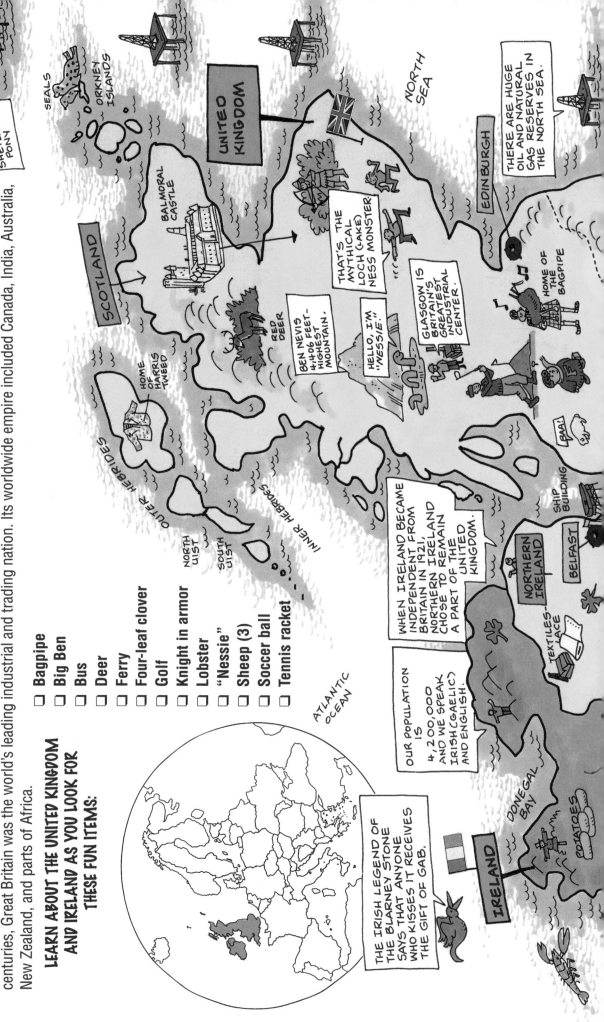

SHETLAND ISLANDS

HOME OF THE SHETLAND PONY

BAA!

SEALS

ORKNEY ISLANDS

NORTH SEA

UNITED KINGDOM

THERE ARE HUGE OIL AND NATURAL GAS RESERVES IN THE NORTH SEA.

EDINBURGH

BALMORAL CASTLE

SCOTLAND

THAT'S THE MYTHICAL LOCH (LAKE) NESS MONSTER.

HOME OF THE BAGPIPE

BEN NEVIS 4,406 FEET— HIGHEST MOUNTAIN.

HELLO, I'M "NESSIE"!

GLASGOW IS BRITAIN'S GREATEST INDUSTRIAL CENTER.

RED DEER

HOME OF HARRIS TWEED

OUTER HEBRIDES

NORTH UIST

SOUTH UIST

INNER HEBRIDES

BAA!

SHIP BUILDING

BELFAST

NORTHERN IRELAND

WHEN IRELAND BECAME INDEPENDENT FROM BRITAIN IN 1921, NORTHERN IRELAND CHOSE TO REMAIN A PART OF THE UNITED KINGDOM.

TEXTILES-LACE

OUR POPULATION IS 4,200,000 AND WE SPEAK IRISH (GAELIC) AND ENGLISH.

ATLANTIC OCEAN

DONEGAL BAY

POTATOES

IRELAND

THE IRISH LEGEND OF THE BLARNEY STONE SAYS THAT ANYONE WHO KISSES IT RECEIVES THE GIFT OF GAB.

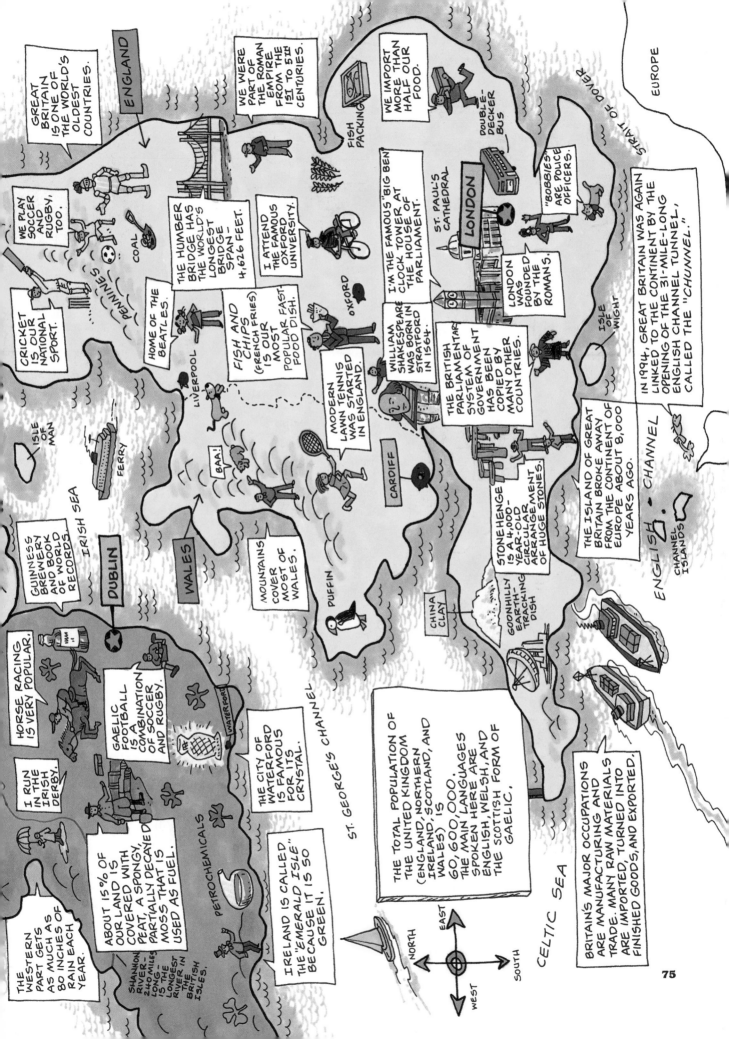

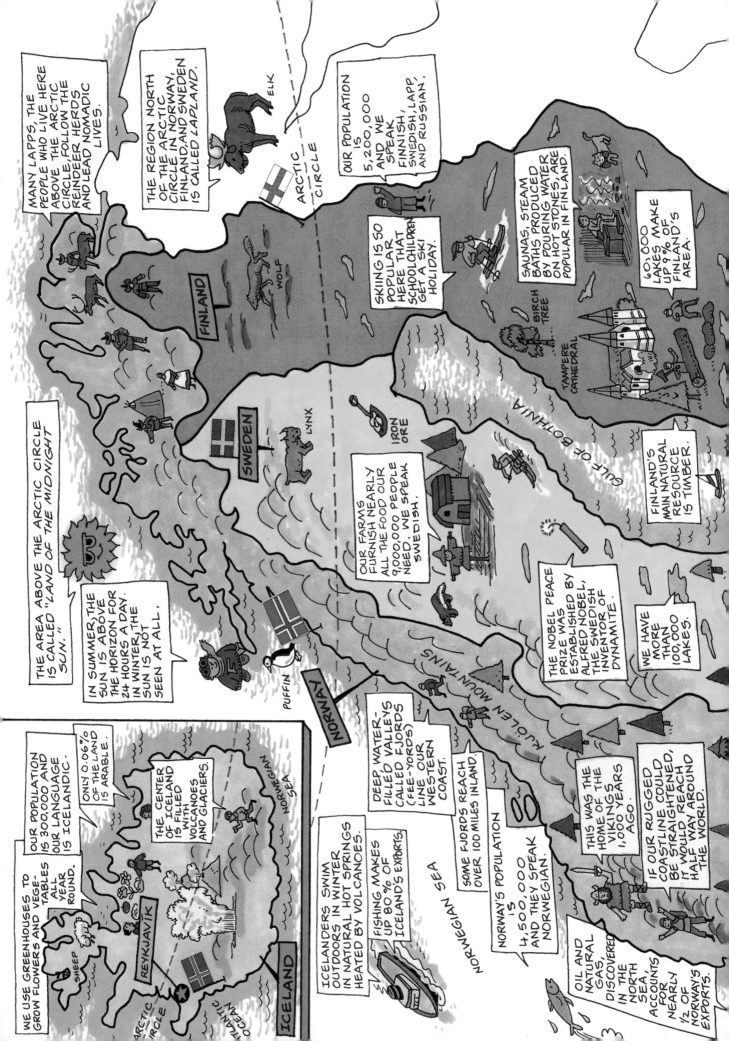

SCANDINAVIA

The peninsular countries of Norway, Sweden, and Denmark form the region known as Scandinavia. Most geographers also include Finland and Iceland in that region. Many Scandinavians are descendants of the seafaring Vikings, who lived in this region about a thousand years ago. The land is rich in natural resources, and Scandinavians enjoy one of the highest standards of living in the world.

LEARN ABOUT SCANDINAVIA AS YOU LOOK FOR THESE FUN ITEMS:

- ☐ Ax
- ☐ Birch tree
- ☐ Chef
- ☐ Dynamite
- ☐ Elk
- ☐ Flowers (2)

- ☐ Geyser
- ☐ Legos
- ☐ Lynx
- ☐ Pig
- ☐ Puffin
- ☐ Scarecrow

- ☐ Sheep (2)
- ☐ Skiers (2)
- ☐ Tepee
- ☐ Viking
- ☐ Volcanoes (2)
- ☐ Wolf

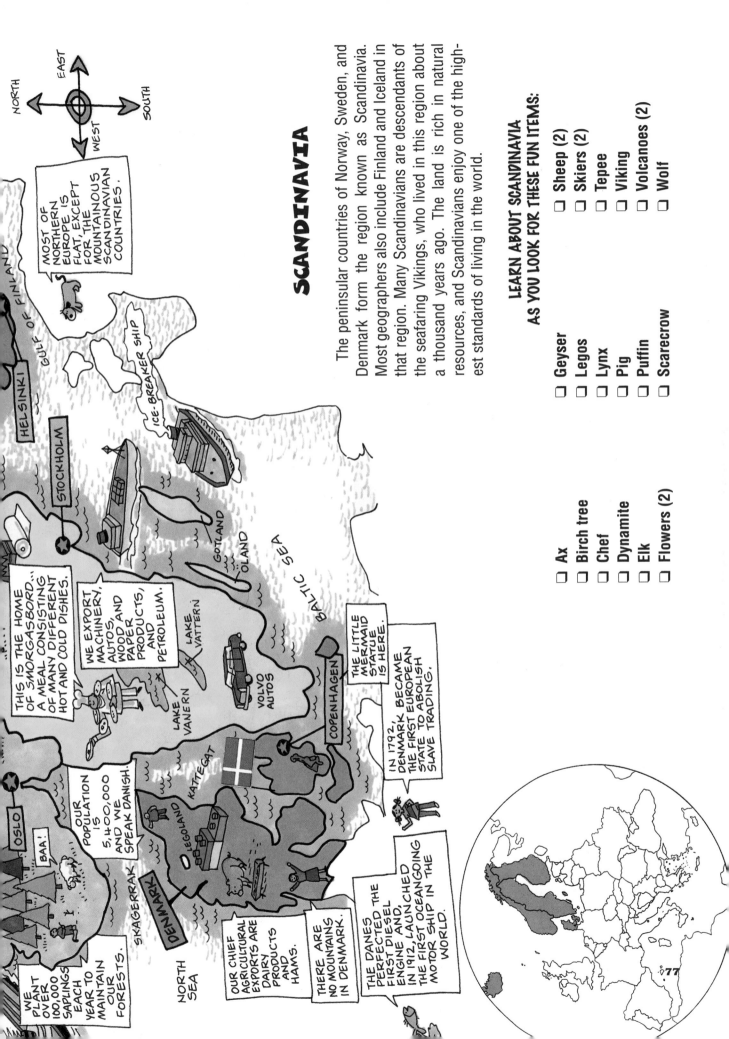

NORTH
EAST
SOUTH
WEST

MOST OF NORTHERN EUROPE IS FLAT, EXCEPT FOR THE MOUNTAINOUS SCANDINAVIAN COUNTRIES.

GULF OF FINLAND

HELSINKI

ICE-BREAKER SHIP

STOCKHOLM

GOTLAND

OLAND

BALTIC SEA

THIS IS THE HOME OF SMORGASBORD... A MEAL CONSISTING OF MANY DIFFERENT HOT AND COLD DISHES.

WE EXPORT MACHINERY, AUTOS, WOOD AND PAPER PRODUCTS, AND PETROLEUM.

LAKE VATTERN

LAKE VANERN

VOLVO AUTOS

COPENHAGEN

THE LITTLE MERMAID STATUE IS HERE.

IN 1792, DENMARK BECAME THE FIRST EUROPEAN STATE TO ABOLISH SLAVE TRADING.

KATTEGAT

LEGOLAND

OSLO

BAA!

OUR POPULATION IS 5,400,000 AND WE SPEAK DANISH.

SKAGERRAK

DENMARK

NORTH SEA

OUR CHIEF AGRICULTURAL EXPORTS ARE DAIRY PRODUCTS AND HAMS.

THERE ARE NO MOUNTAINS IN DENMARK.

THE DANES PERFECTED THE FIRST DIESEL ENGINE AND, IN 1912, LAUNCHED THE FIRST OCEANGOING MOTOR SHIP IN THE WORLD.

WE PLANT OVER 100,000 SAPLINGS EACH YEAR TO MAINTAIN OUR FORESTS.

77

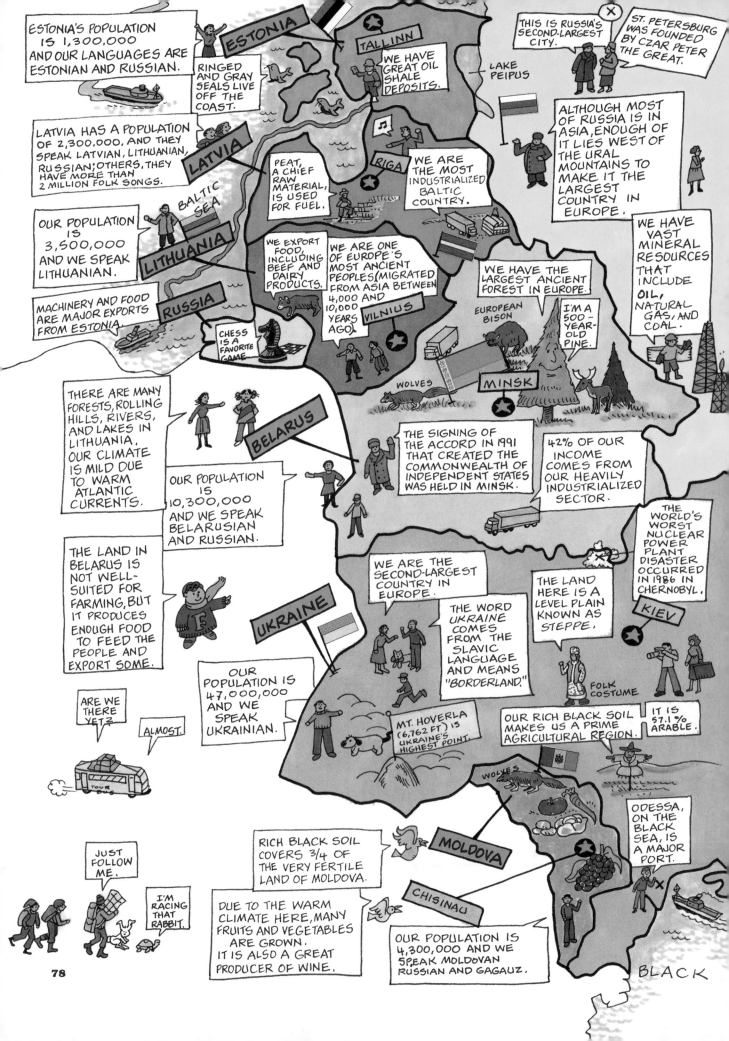

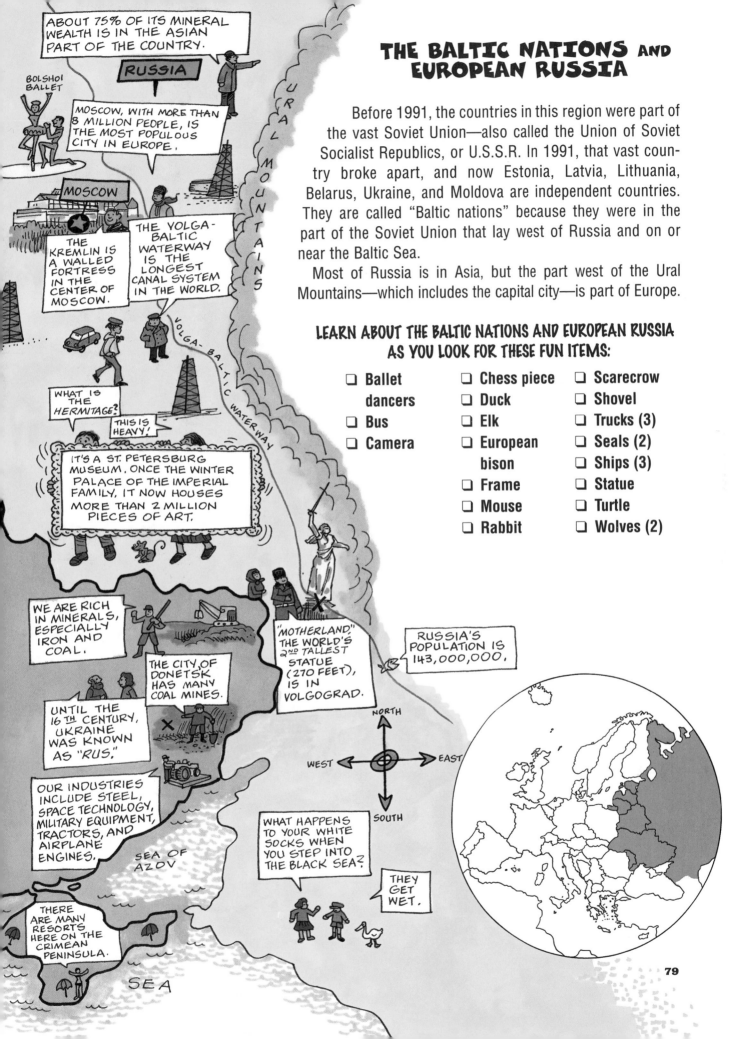

THE BALTIC NATIONS AND EUROPEAN RUSSIA

Before 1991, the countries in this region were part of the vast Soviet Union—also called the Union of Soviet Socialist Republics, or U.S.S.R. In 1991, that vast country broke apart, and now Estonia, Latvia, Lithuania, Belarus, Ukraine, and Moldova are independent countries. They are called "Baltic nations" because they were in the part of the Soviet Union that lay west of Russia and on or near the Baltic Sea.

Most of Russia is in Asia, but the part west of the Ural Mountains—which includes the capital city—is part of Europe.

LEARN ABOUT THE BALTIC NATIONS AND EUROPEAN RUSSIA AS YOU LOOK FOR THESE FUN ITEMS:

- ❏ Ballet dancers
- ❏ Bus
- ❏ Camera
- ❏ Chess piece
- ❏ Duck
- ❏ Elk
- ❏ European bison
- ❏ Frame
- ❏ Mouse
- ❏ Rabbit
- ❏ Scarecrow
- ❏ Shovel
- ❏ Trucks (3)
- ❏ Seals (2)
- ❏ Ships (3)
- ❏ Statue
- ❏ Turtle
- ❏ Wolves (2)

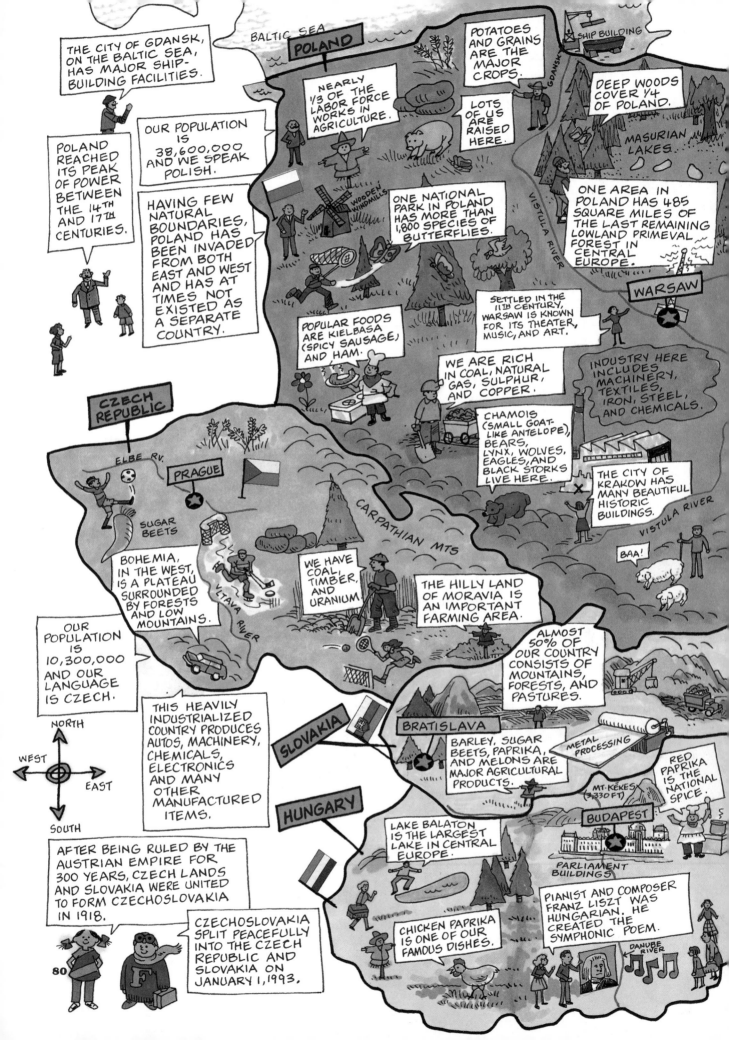

POLAND, CZECH REPUBLIC, SLOVAKIA, AND HUNGARY

When World War II ended in 1945, many countries in Eastern Europe came under the control of the Soviet Union. When the Soviet Union broke apart in 1991, the people in Poland, Czechoslovakia, and Hungary once again took charge of their own governments. In 1993, Czechoslovakia split into two independent countries, the Czech Republic and Slovakia.

LEARN ABOUT POLAND, CZECH REPUBLC, SLOVAKIA, AND HUNGARY AS YOU LOOK FOR THESE FUN ITEMS:

- ❏ Barn
- ❏ Bear
- ❏ Bird
- ❏ Bison
- ❏ Butterflies (4)
- ❏ Carrot
- ❏ Cooks (3)
- ❏ Flower
- ❏ Hockey player
- ❏ Music notes
- ❏ Pigs (2)
- ❏ Radio tower
- ❏ Sausage
- ❏ Scarecrows (5)
- ❏ Sheep
- ❏ Tennis ball
- ❏ Tourists
- ❏ Truck
- ❏ Windmill
- ❏ Woolly mammoth

THE NORTHEASTERN REGION IS DENSE WITH TALL TREES AND LAKES.

BUG RIVER

EUROPEAN BISON

PALACE OF CULTURE

OJCOW NATIONAL PARK IN THE SOUTH HAS 50 CAVES WHERE PREHISTORIC PEOPLE LIVED.

REMAINS OF PREHISTORIC MAMMOTHS HAVE ALSO BEEN FOUND THERE.

OUR POPULATION IS 5,400,000 AND OUR LANGUAGES ARE SLOVAK AND HUNGARIAN.

GOULASH, A TRADITIONAL HUNGARIAN DISH, IS A STEW OF MEAT, POTATOES, ONIONS, AND PAPRIKA (A SPICE MADE FROM SWEET RED PEPPERS), AND IS MY FAVORITE DISH TO MAKE.

WE'RE NOT LOST!

BECAUSE MOST OF OUR LAND IS FERTILE, HUNGARIANS PRODUCE ENOUGH FOOD TO FEED THE COUNTRY AND SELL ABROAD.

OUR POPULATION IS 10,100,000.

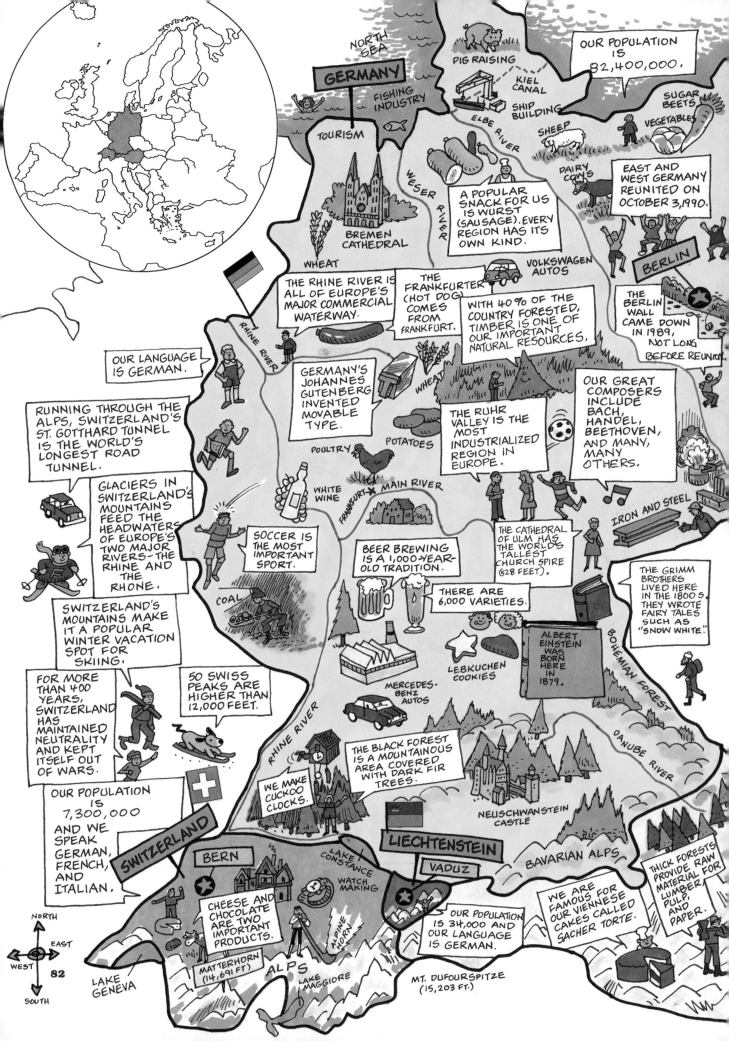

GERMANY

NORTH SEA

PIG RAISING

OUR POPULATION IS 82,400,000.

KIEL CANAL

SHIP BUILDING

ELBE RIVER

SHEEP

SUGAR BEETS

VEGETABLES

FISHING INDUSTRY

TOURISM

WESER RIVER

DAIRY COWS

EAST AND WEST GERMANY REUNITED ON OCTOBER 3, 1990.

BREMEN CATHEDRAL

A POPULAR SNACK FOR US IS WURST (SAUSAGE). EVERY REGION HAS ITS OWN KIND.

WHEAT

BERLIN

THE RHINE RIVER IS ALL OF EUROPE'S MAJOR COMMERCIAL WATERWAY.

THE FRANKFURTER (HOT DOG) COMES FROM FRANKFURT.

VOLKSWAGEN AUTOS

THE BERLIN WALL CAME DOWN IN 1989, NOT LONG BEFORE REUNION.

RHINE RIVER

WITH 40% OF THE COUNTRY FORESTED, TIMBER IS ONE OF OUR IMPORTANT NATURAL RESOURCES.

OUR LANGUAGE IS GERMAN.

GERMANY'S JOHANNES GUTENBERG INVENTED MOVABLE TYPE.

WHEAT

OUR GREAT COMPOSERS INCLUDE BACH, HANDEL, BEETHOVEN, AND MANY, MANY OTHERS.

RUNNING THROUGH THE ALPS, SWITZERLAND'S ST. GOTTHARD TUNNEL IS THE WORLD'S LONGEST ROAD TUNNEL.

THE RUHR VALLEY IS THE MOST INDUSTRIALIZED REGION IN EUROPE.

POULTRY

POTATOES

IRON AND STEEL

GLACIERS IN SWITZERLAND'S MOUNTAINS FEED THE HEADWATERS OF EUROPE'S TWO MAJOR RIVERS—THE RHINE AND THE RHONE.

WHITE WINE

FRANKFURT

MAIN RIVER

SOCCER IS THE MOST IMPORTANT SPORT.

BEER BREWING IS A 1,000-YEAR-OLD TRADITION.

THE CATHEDRAL OF ULM HAS THE WORLD'S TALLEST CHURCH SPIRE (528 FEET).

THE GRIMM BROTHERS LIVED HERE IN THE 1800'S. THEY WROTE FAIRY TALES SUCH AS "SNOW WHITE."

SWITZERLAND'S MOUNTAINS MAKE IT A POPULAR WINTER VACATION SPOT FOR SKIING.

COAL

THERE ARE 6,000 VARIETIES.

LEBKUCHEN COOKIES

ALBERT EINSTEIN WAS BORN HERE IN 1879.

BOHEMIAN FOREST

FOR MORE THAN 400 YEARS, SWITZERLAND HAS MAINTAINED NEUTRALITY AND KEPT ITSELF OUT OF WARS.

50 SWISS PEAKS ARE HIGHER THAN 12,000 FEET.

MERCEDES-BENZ AUTOS

RHINE RIVER

THE BLACK FOREST IS A MOUNTAINOUS AREA COVERED WITH DARK FIR TREES.

DANUBE RIVER

OUR POPULATION IS 7,300,000 AND WE SPEAK GERMAN, FRENCH, AND ITALIAN.

WE MAKE CUCKOO CLOCKS.

NEUSCHWANSTEIN CASTLE

SWITZERLAND

BERN

LIECHTENSTEIN

VADUZ

BAVARIAN ALPS

THICK FORESTS PROVIDE RAW MATERIAL FOR LUMBER, PULP, AND PAPER.

LAKE CONSTANCE

WATCH MAKING

CHEESE AND CHOCOLATE ARE TWO IMPORTANT PRODUCTS.

OUR POPULATION IS 34,000 AND OUR LANGUAGE IS GERMAN.

WE ARE FAMOUS FOR OUR VIENNESE CAKES CALLED SACHER TORTE.

ALPINE HORN

NORTH

EAST

WEST

SOUTH

82

MATTERHORN (14,691 FT.)

ALPS

LAKE MAGGIORE

LAKE GENEVA

MT. DUFOURSPITZE (15,203 FT.)

GERMANY, SWITZERLAND, LIECHTENSTEIN, AND AUSTRIA

The countries of Germany, Switzerland, Liechtenstein, and Austria lie in an area sometimes known as central Europe. From north to south, this region's landscape changes from marshy plains to snowcapped moutains. It is crossed by two of Europe's longest rivers—the Rhine and the Danube—and by the Alps, the famous mountain range that is the longest and highest mountain range in western Europe.

LEARN ABOUT GERMANY, SWITZERLAND, LIECHTENSTEIN, AND AUSTRIA AS YOU LOOK FOR THESE FUN ITEMS:

- ❑ Alpine horn blower
- ❑ Automobiles (3)
- ❑ Ax
- ❑ Berlin Wall
- ❑ Books (3)
- ❑ Cake
- ❑ Carrot
- ❑ Chicken
- ❑ Coal miner
- ❑ Cookies
- ❑ Cows (2)
- ❑ Cuckoo clock
- ❑ Dogs (2)
- ❑ Great white heron
- ❑ Horse
- ❑ Hot dogs
- ❑ Pigs (2)
- ❑ Soccer ball
- ❑ Telescope
- ❑ Tuba
- ❑ Watch

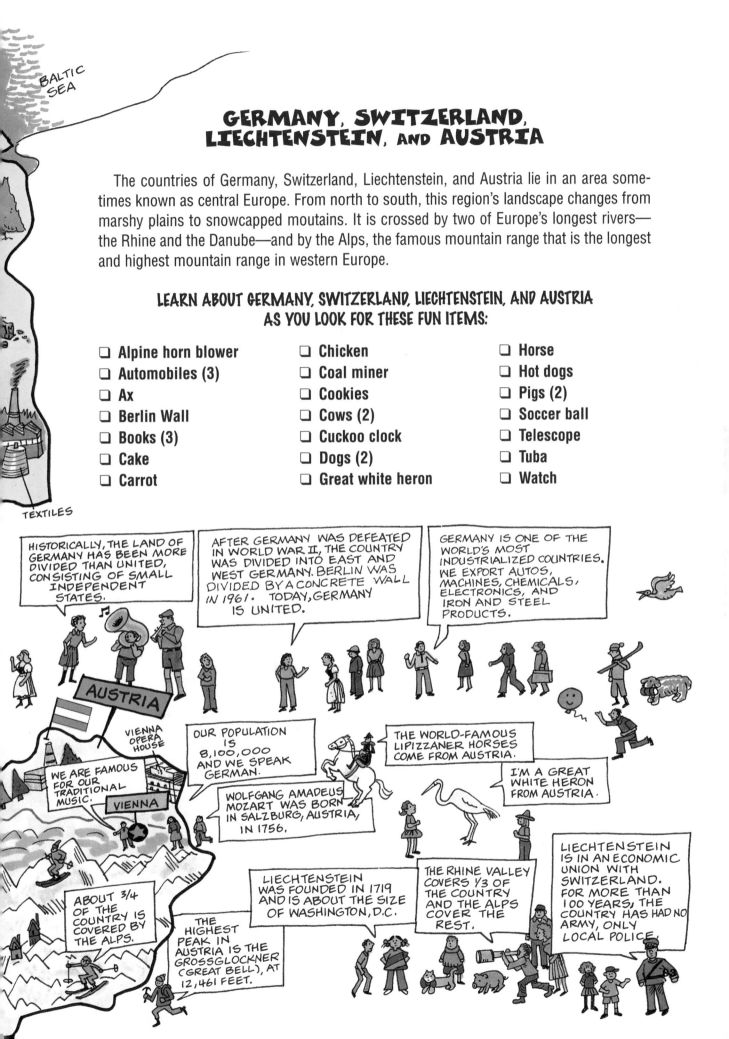

BALTIC SEA

TEXTILES

HISTORICALLY, THE LAND OF GERMANY HAS BEEN MORE DIVIDED THAN UNITED, CONSISTING OF SMALL INDEPENDENT STATES.

AFTER GERMANY WAS DEFEATED IN WORLD WAR II, THE COUNTRY WAS DIVIDED INTO EAST AND WEST GERMANY. BERLIN WAS DIVIDED BY A CONCRETE WALL IN 1961. TODAY, GERMANY IS UNITED.

GERMANY IS ONE OF THE WORLD'S MOST INDUSTRIALIZED COUNTRIES. WE EXPORT AUTOS, MACHINES, CHEMICALS, ELECTRONICS, AND IRON AND STEEL PRODUCTS.

AUSTRIA

VIENNA OPERA HOUSE

WE ARE FAMOUS FOR OUR TRADITIONAL MUSIC.

VIENNA

OUR POPULATION IS 8,100,000 AND WE SPEAK GERMAN.

WOLFGANG AMADEUS MOZART WAS BORN IN SALZBURG, AUSTRIA, IN 1756.

THE WORLD-FAMOUS LIPIZZANER HORSES COME FROM AUSTRIA.

I'M A GREAT WHITE HERON FROM AUSTRIA.

LIECHTENSTEIN IS IN AN ECONOMIC UNION WITH SWITZERLAND. FOR MORE THAN 100 YEARS, THE COUNTRY HAS HAD NO ARMY, ONLY LOCAL POLICE.

ABOUT 3/4 OF THE COUNTRY IS COVERED BY THE ALPS.

THE HIGHEST PEAK IN AUSTRIA IS THE GROSSGLOCKNER (GREAT BELL), AT 12,461 FEET.

LIECHTENSTEIN WAS FOUNDED IN 1719 AND IS ABOUT THE SIZE OF WASHINGTON, D.C.

THE RHINE VALLEY COVERS 1/3 OF THE COUNTRY AND THE ALPS COVER THE REST.

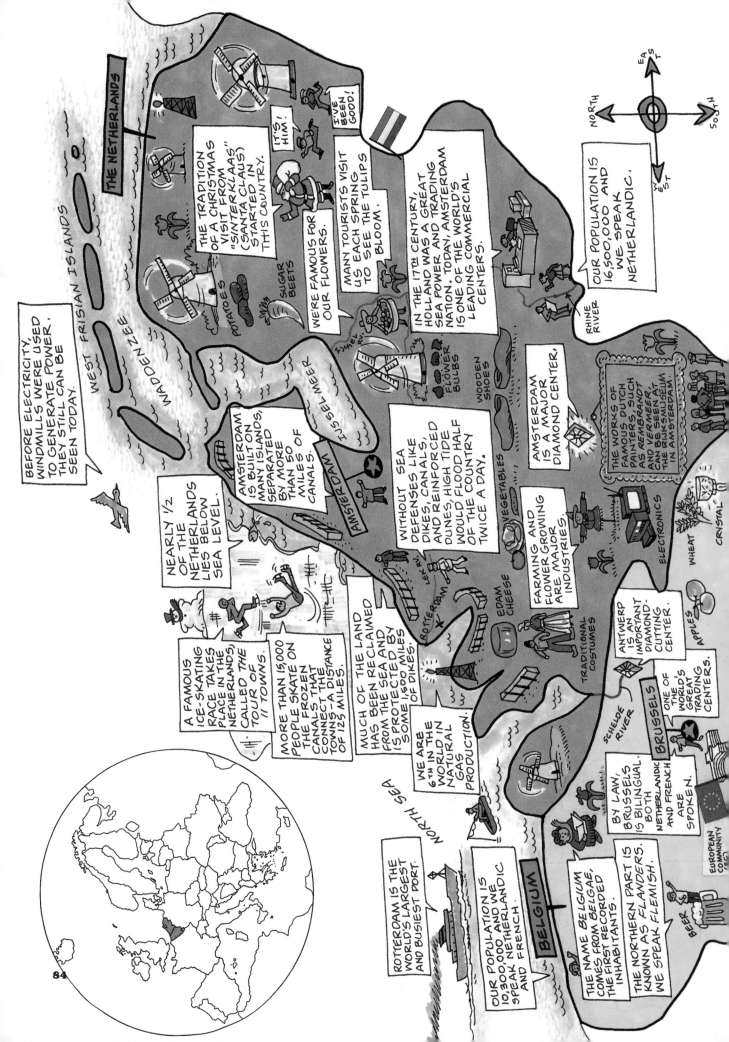

THE NETHERLANDS, BELGIUM, AND LUXEMBOURG

The Netherlands is situated on very low-lying land. With an average altitude of only 37 feet, it is the flattest country in the world! (The word *Netherlands* means "the lowlands.") Belgium, though not as flat, also sits low. The two lands are known as "the Low Countries."

Those two countries plus Luxembourg are sometimes referred to as "Benelux." Their small size and large populations make this region one of the most densely populated areas in Europe.

LEARN ABOUT THE NETHERLANDS, BELGIUM, AND LUXEMBOURG AS YOU LOOK FOR THESE FUN ITEMS:

- ☐ Crystal
- ☐ Deer
- ☐ Diamonds (2)
- ☐ Fishing pole
- ☐ Frame
- ☐ Grapes
- ☐ Pig
- ☐ Santa Claus
- ☐ Shovel
- ☐ Soccer ball
- ☐ Telescope
- ☐ Tulips (5)
- ☐ TV set
- ☐ Waffle
- ☐ Windmills (5)
- ☐ Wooden shoes (2 pairs)

FRANCE AND MONACO

France is one of the oldest countries in Europe. It also is one of the world's leading countries in terms of culture, historic and political influence, industry, and agriculture. The capital and cultural center is the city of Paris, nicknamed "the City of Light."

At France's southeastern corner lies Monaco, one of the world's smallest nations. (*Monaco* is also the name of its capital city.)

LEARN ABOUT FRANCE AND MONACO AS YOU LOOK FOR THESE FUN ITEMS:

- ❑ Apples (2)
- ❑ Artichoke
- ❑ Artist
- ❑ Automobile
- ❑ Chef
- ❑ Cyclist
- ❑ Dice
- ❑ Eels
- ❑ Eiffel Tower
- ❑ Geese (2)
- ❑ Mouse
- ❑ Musician
- ❑ Mustard
- ❑ Napoleon
- ❑ Paper airplane
- ❑ Perfume bottle
- ❑ Pig
- ❑ Red balloon
- ❑ Skier
- ❑ Snail
- ❑ Soccer ball
- ❑ Umbrellas (2)
- ❑ Walnuts

ENGLISH CHANNEL

I'M ALWAYS CRABBY.

FRANCE

THE NORMANDY REGION IS KNOWN FOR ITS DAIRY PRODUCTS AND APPLES.

FRENCH CHEFS AND FRENCH COOKING ARE KNOWN THROUGHOUT THE WORLD.

NORMANDY REGION

THERE ARE MANY BEAUTIFUL CHATEAUX (COUNTRY PALACES) ALONG THE LOIRE VALLEY.

THIS IS FRANCE'S LONGEST RIVER.

LOIRE RV.

MORE THAN 3,000 MILES OF CANALS LINK THE RIVERS OF FRANCE.

ATLANTIC OCEAN

WE'RE EELS.

THE TGV TRAIN CAN GO 168 MPH, MAKING IT ONE OF THE FASTEST TRAINS IN THE WORLD.

BRANDY   BEEF CATTLE

BAY OF BISCAY

WE EXPORT CLOTHING, FOOD, CHEMICALS, AUTOS, AND MANY OTHER PRODUCTS.

WE ARE A LEADER IN FASHION AND PERFUME MANUFACTURING.

TOBACCO

WINE HAS BEEN MADE IN FRANCE SINCE ROMAN TIMES.

WALNUTS

GARONNE RV.

OIL

PYRENEES MTS

NORTH

WEST   EAST

SOUTH

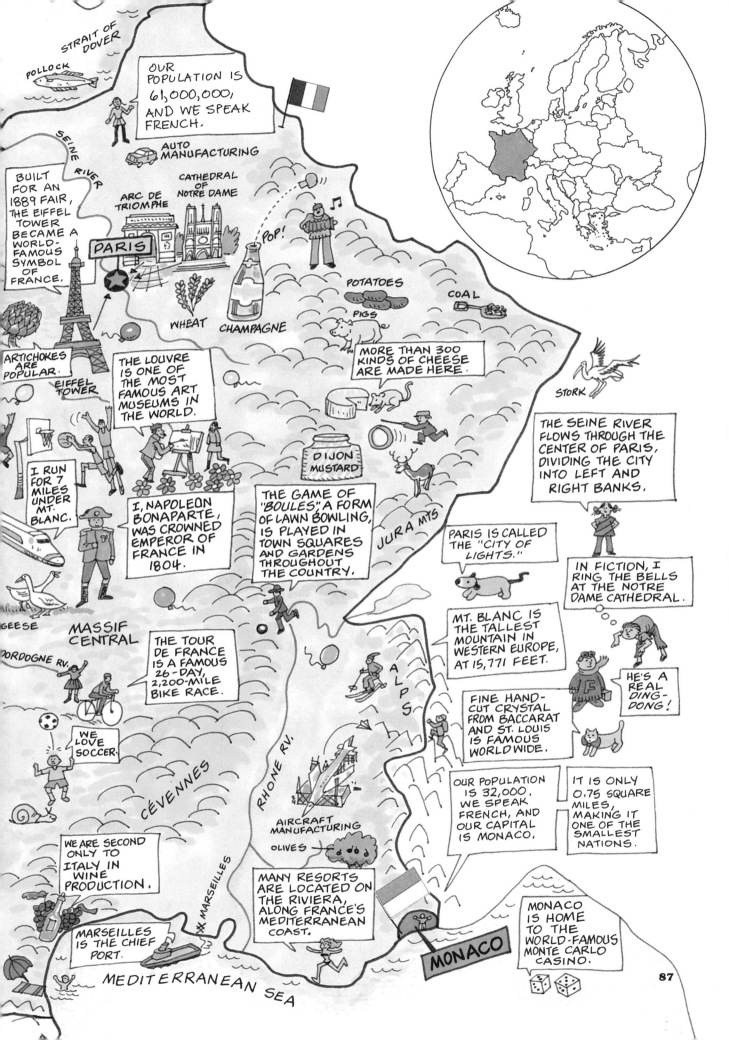

THE IBERIAN PENINSULA

Spain, Portugal, and Andorra share a piece of land called the Iberian Peninsula. (A *peninsula* is a land area with water on all sides except for a neck of land connected to a larger landmass.) Spain and Portugal have long seafaring histories. Their explorers and settlers once ruled empires in Africa, Asia, North America, and South America. Tiny Andorra, tucked into an area of the Pyrenees Mountains, is landlocked.

Today, fishing, farming, and tourism are major industries in Spain and Portugal. More than 60 million tourists each year visit their historical cities and sun-drenched beaches.

LEARN ABOUT THE IBERIAN PENINSULA AS YOU LOOK FOR THESE FUN ITEMS:

- ☐ **Anchovies**
- ☐ **Bottles (5)**
- ☐ **Brown bear**
- ☐ **Bulls (3)**
- ☐ **Cheese**
- ☐ **Cork**
- ☐ **Guitar**
- ☐ **Ibex**
- ☐ **Olive tree**
- ☐ **Skier**
- ☐ **Sunflowers (4)**
- ☐ **Umbrellas (3)**
- ☐ **Windmill**
- ☐ **Windsurfers (3)**

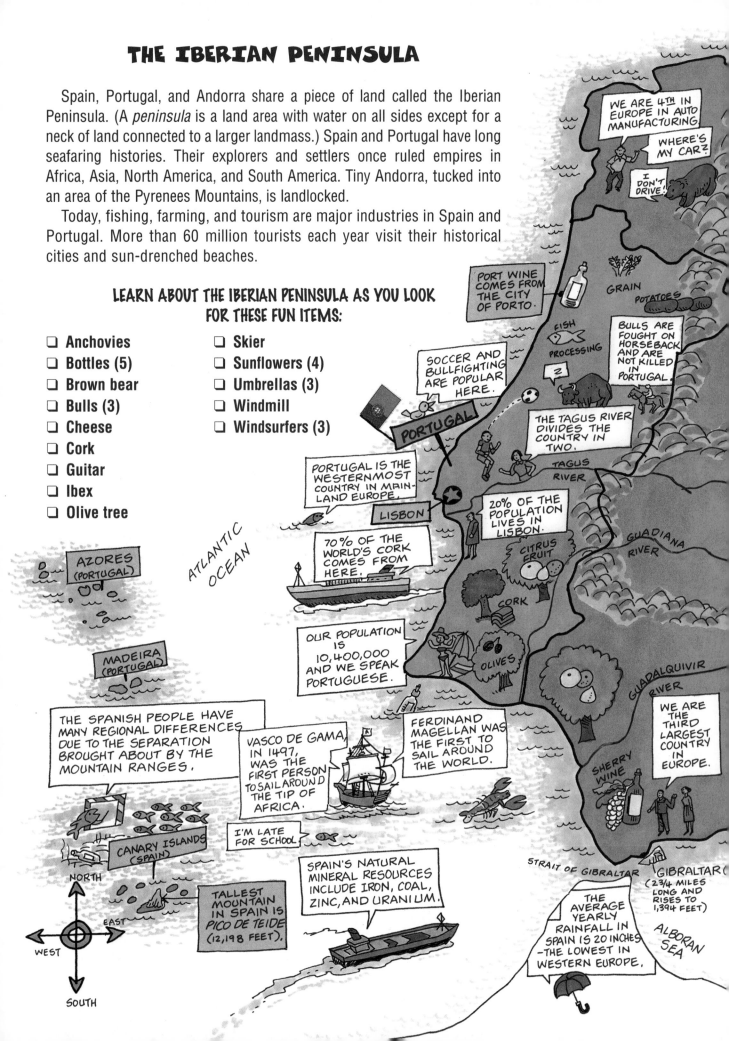

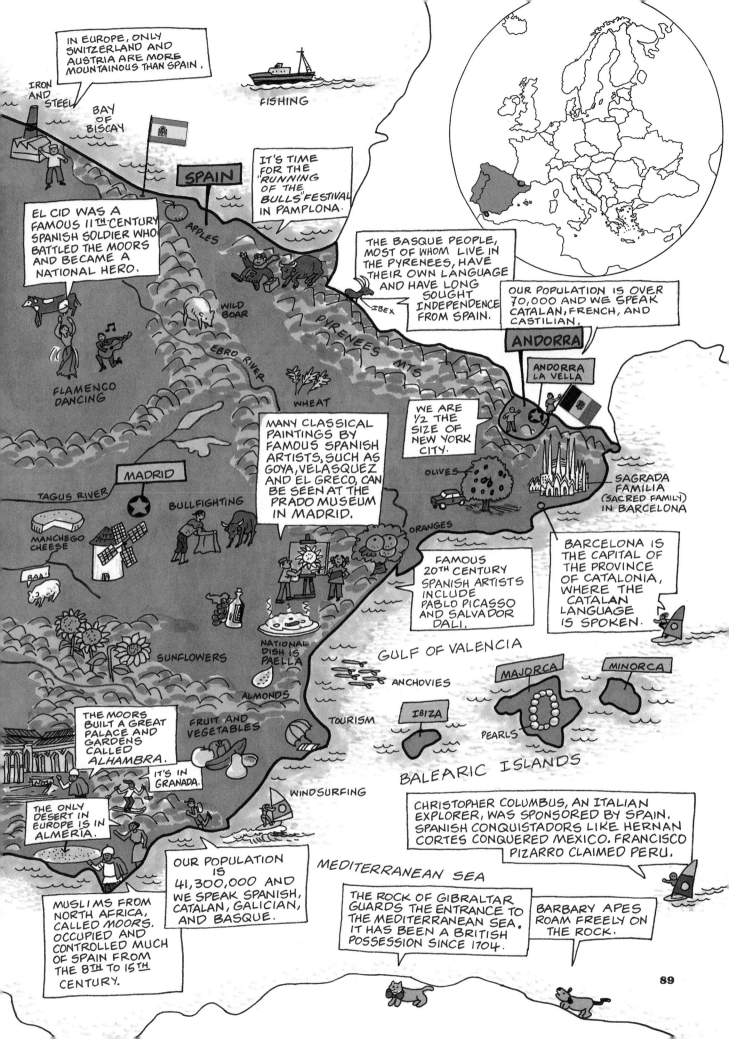

AT ITS HEIGHT IN THE 2ND CENTURY A.D., THE ROMAN EMPIRE EXTENDED FROM SCOTLAND TO THE MIDDLE EAST.

FROM THE 2ND CENTURY B.C. UNTIL THE 5TH CENTURY A.D., ROME WAS AT THE CENTER OF THE WESTERN WORLD.

ADRIATIC SEA

OCTOPUSES

CRABS

ITALY IS THE WORLD'S LEADING WINE PRODUCER.

WE ARE KNOWN FOR OUR OLIVE OIL, PASTA, CHEESE, TOMATOES, AND WINE.

THERE ARE NO AUTOS IN VENICE. TRAVEL IS ONLY BY FOOT, GONDOLA, WATERBUS, OR MOTORBOAT.

TOBACCO

PIZZA

VENICE IS A CITY OF ISLANDS, CRISSCROSSED BY CANALS AND FOOTBRIDGES.

ST. MARKS SQUARE IN VENICE

VENETIAN GONDOLIER

A FAMOUS HORSE RACE, CALLED THE PALIO, TAKES PLACE IN THE TOWN SQUARE OF THE ANCIENT CITY OF SIENA.

ST. PETER'S BASILICA IS THE WORLD'S LARGEST CHRISTIAN CHURCH.

ROME

THE COLOSSEUM (ROME)

OUR POPULATION IS 58,100,000 AND WE SPEAK ITALIAN.

SAN MARINO

OUR POPULATION IS 30,000. WE SPEAK ITALIAN.

VATICAN CITY

APENNINES MTS.

LAKE GARDA

AT 405 MILES, THE PO RIVER IS THE LONGEST IN ITALY.

PO RIVER

WE ARE THE WORLD'S LEADING PRODUCER OF MARBLE, BUT HAVE FEW OTHER NATURAL RESOURCES.

THE RENAISSANCE —A REBIRTH OF ART, SCIENCE, LITERATURE, AND LEARNING— BEGAN IN FLORENCE IN THE 15TH CENTURY.

X LEANING TOWER OF PISA

LAKE COMO

ALPS

WAIT FOR ME!

LAKE MAGGIORE

ITALY

THE CITY OF MILAN IS ONE OF THE LEADING FINANCIAL AND MANUFACTURING CENTERS OF EUROPE.

X MILAN

OPERA WAS FIRST PERFORMED IN ITALY.

CARRARA X

LIGURIAN SEA

TYRRHENIAN SEA

MANY SHEEP ARE RAISED ON THE STONY, MOUNTAINOUS ISLAND OF SARDINIA.

SQUID

50 MILLION TOURISTS VISIT ITALY'S MUSEUMS, MONUMENTS, FAMOUS CITIES, AND RESORTS EACH YEAR.

AVANTI! (FORWARD)

OLIVE TREES

NORTH
EAST
WEST
SOUTH

SOME OF THE FAMOUS ITALIANS OF THE RENAISSANCE ERA WERE MICHELANGELO, A PAINTER AND SCULPTOR; GALILEO, AN ASTRONOMER; AND LEONARDO DA VINCI, WHO WAS NOT ONLY AN ARTIST, BUT A SCIENTIST AND INVENTOR.

PAINT MY PICTURE.

SARDINIA

90

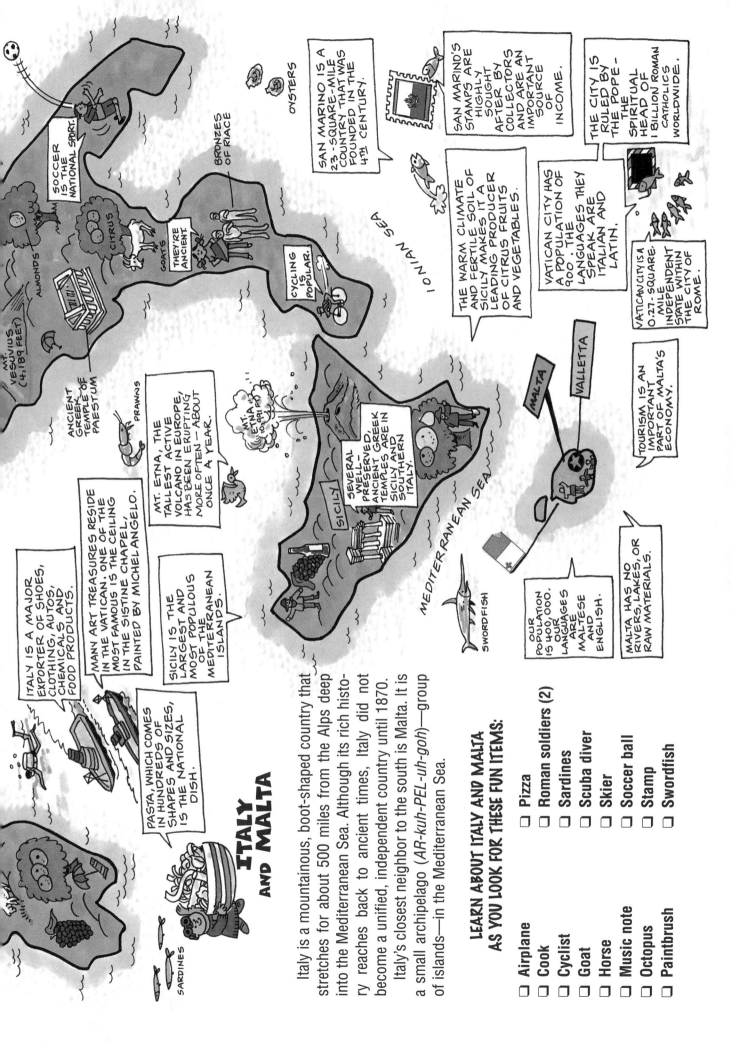

ITALY AND MALTA

Italy is a mountainous, boot-shaped country that stretches for about 500 miles from the Alps deep into the Mediterranean Sea. Although its rich history reaches back to ancient times, Italy did not become a unified, independent country until 1870. Italy's closest neighbor to the south is Malta. It is a small archipelago (AR-kuh-PEL-uh-goh)—group of islands—in the Mediterranean Sea.

LEARN ABOUT ITALY AND MALTA AS YOU LOOK FOR THESE FUN ITEMS:

- ☐ Airplane
- ☐ Cook
- ☐ Cyclist
- ☐ Goat
- ☐ Horse
- ☐ Music note
- ☐ Octopus
- ☐ Paintbrush
- ☐ Pizza
- ☐ Roman soldiers (2)
- ☐ Sardines
- ☐ Scuba diver
- ☐ Skier
- ☐ Soccer ball
- ☐ Stamp
- ☐ Swordfish

SOCCER IS THE NATIONAL SPORT.

OYSTERS

SAN MARINO IS A 23-SQUARE-MILE COUNTRY THAT WAS FOUNDED IN THE 4TH CENTURY.

SAN MARINO'S STAMPS ARE HIGHLY SOUGHT AFTER BY COLLECTORS AND ARE AN IMPORTANT SOURCE OF INCOME.

THE CITY IS RULED BY THE POPE — THE SPIRITUAL HEAD OF 1 BILLION ROMAN CATHOLICS WORLDWIDE.

BRONZES OF RIACE

CITRUS

GOATS

THEY'RE ANCIENT.

CYCLING IS POPULAR.

IONIAN SEA

THE WARM CLIMATE AND FERTILE SOIL OF SICILY MAKES IT A LEADING PRODUCER OF CITRUS FRUITS AND VEGETABLES.

VATICAN CITY HAS A POPULATION OF 900. THE LANGUAGES THEY SPEAK ARE ITALIAN AND LATIN.

VATICAN CITY IS A 0.27-SQUARE-MILE INDEPENDENT STATE WITHIN THE CITY OF ROME.

MT. VESUVIUS (4,189 FEET)

ALMONDS

ANCIENT GREEK TEMPLE OF PAESTUM

PRAWNS

MT. ETNA, THE TALLEST ACTIVE VOLCANO IN EUROPE, HAS BEEN ERUPTING MORE OFTEN — ABOUT ONCE A YEAR.

MT. ETNA 10,911 FT.

SICILY

SEVERAL WELL-PRESERVED, ANCIENT GREEK TEMPLES ARE IN SICILY AND SOUTHERN ITALY.

MALTA

VALLETTA

TOURISM IS AN IMPORTANT PART OF MALTA'S ECONOMY.

MEDITERRANEAN SEA

SWORDFISH

ITALY IS A MAJOR EXPORTER OF SHOES, CLOTHING, AUTOS, CHEMICALS, AND FOOD PRODUCTS.

MANY ART TREASURES RESIDE IN THE VATICAN. ONE OF THE MOST FAMOUS IS THE CEILING IN THE SISTINE CHAPEL, PAINTED BY MICHELANGELO.

SICILY IS THE LARGEST AND MOST POPULOUS OF THE MEDITERRANEAN ISLANDS.

PASTA, WHICH COMES IN HUNDREDS OF SHAPES AND SIZES, IS THE NATIONAL DISH.

OUR POPULATION IS 400,000. OUR LANGUAGES ARE MALTESE AND ENGLISH.

MALTA HAS NO RIVERS, LAKES, OR RAW MATERIALS.

SARDINES

THE BALKAN NATIONS

Much of this part of eastern Europe, known as the Balkans, was ruled by Turkey from the end of the 15th century until 1913. (The name *Balkan* comes from the Balkan Mountains of Bulgaria.) After World War I, several regions were combined to form Yugoslavia. It was heavily influenced by its huge neighbor, the Soviet Union. Soon after the Soviet Union broke apart in 1991, so did Yugoslavia. That land is now five independent countries: Serbia and Montenegro, Slovenia, Croatia, Bosnia and Herzegovina, and Macedonia.

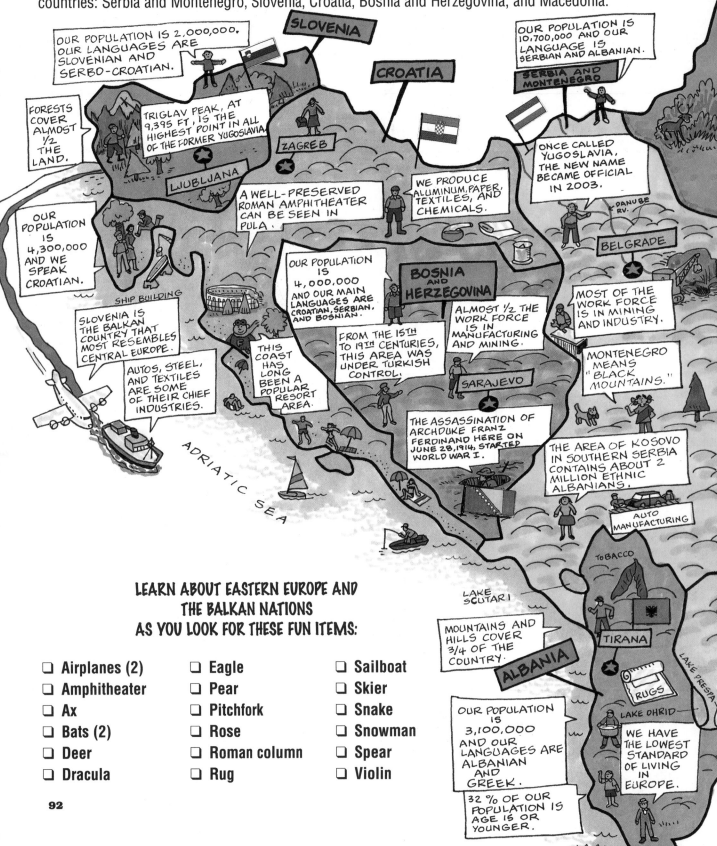

LEARN ABOUT EASTERN EUROPE AND THE BALKAN NATIONS AS YOU LOOK FOR THESE FUN ITEMS:

- ☐ Airplanes (2)
- ☐ Amphitheater
- ☐ Ax
- ☐ Bats (2)
- ☐ Deer
- ☐ Dracula
- ☐ Eagle
- ☐ Pear
- ☐ Pitchfork
- ☐ Rose
- ☐ Roman column
- ☐ Rug
- ☐ Sailboat
- ☐ Skier
- ☐ Snake
- ☐ Snowman
- ☐ Spear
- ☐ Violin

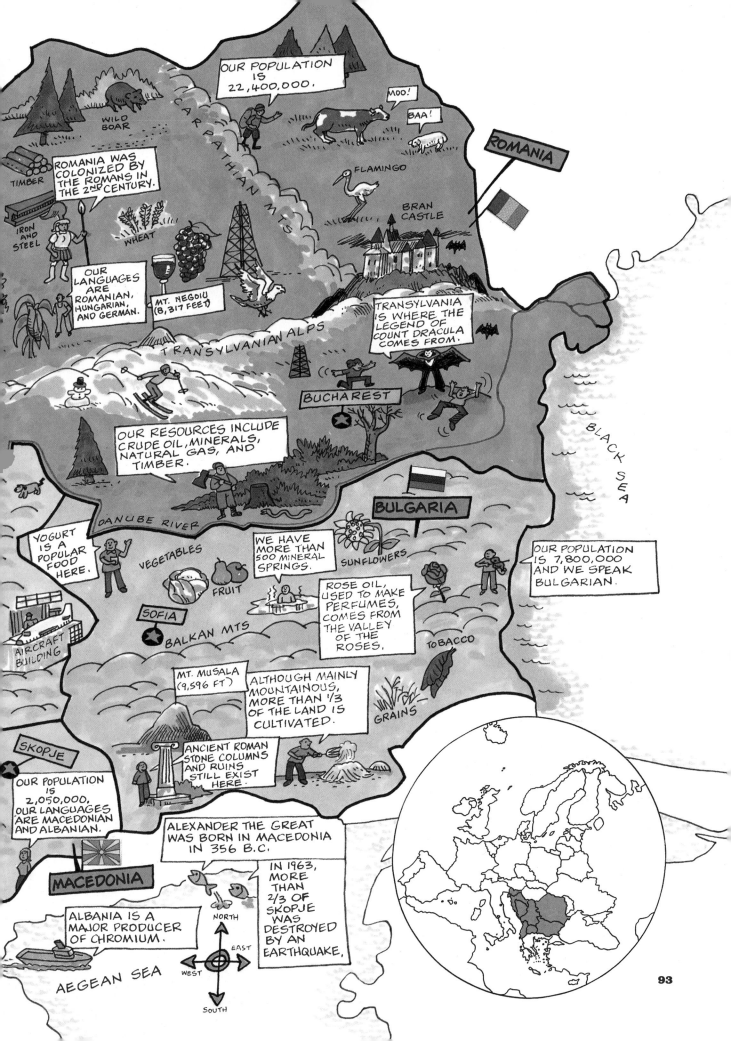

GREECE

The ideals of Western democracy were born in Greece about 2,500 years ago. The art, philosophy, theater, mythology, science, and architecture that flourished there formed the basis of Western civilization.

LEARN ABOUT GREECE AS YOU LOOK FOR THESE FUN ITEMS:
- ☐ Book
- ☐ Cotton
- ☐ Grapes
- ☐ Octopus
- ☐ Olympic torch bearer
- ☐ Sailboat
- ☐ Stone lion
- ☐ Telescope

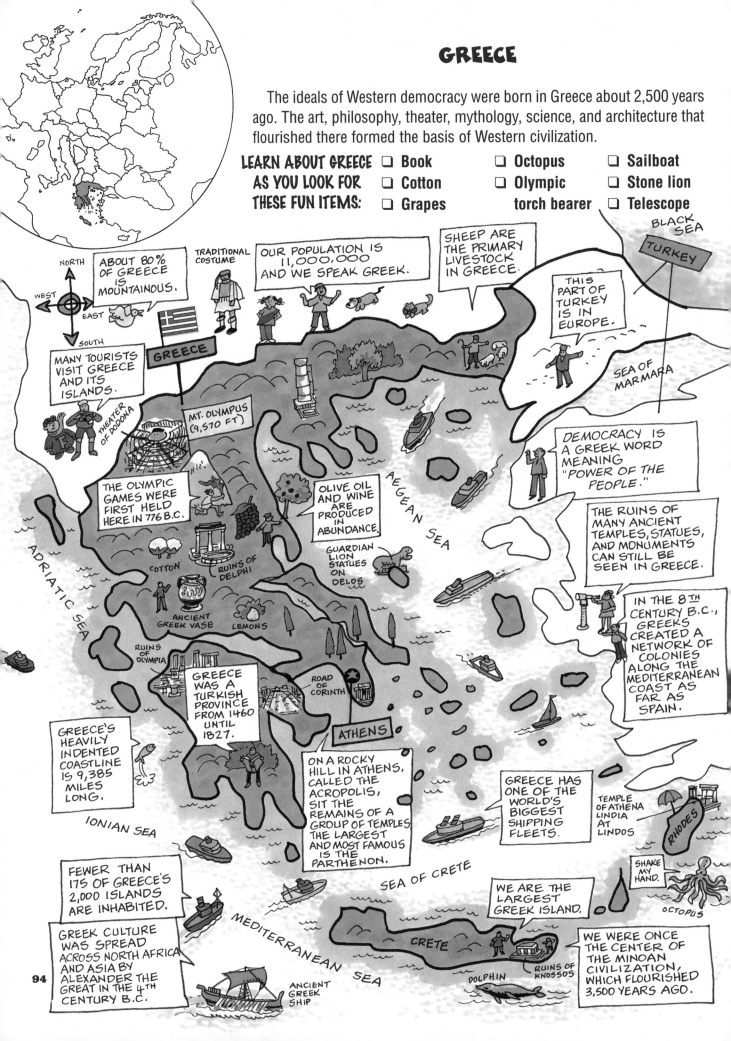

ABOUT 80% OF GREECE IS MOUNTAINOUS.

TRADITIONAL COSTUME

OUR POPULATION IS 11,000,000 AND WE SPEAK GREEK.

SHEEP ARE THE PRIMARY LIVESTOCK IN GREECE.

BLACK SEA

TURKEY

NORTH
WEST
EAST
SOUTH

THIS PART OF TURKEY IS IN EUROPE.

GREECE

MANY TOURISTS VISIT GREECE AND ITS ISLANDS.

THEATER OF DODONA

MT. OLYMPUS (9,570 FT)

SEA OF MARMARA

DEMOCRACY IS A GREEK WORD MEANING "POWER OF THE PEOPLE."

THE OLYMPIC GAMES WERE FIRST HELD HERE IN 776 B.C.

OLIVE OIL AND WINE ARE PRODUCED IN ABUNDANCE.

AEGEAN SEA

THE RUINS OF MANY ANCIENT TEMPLES, STATUES, AND MONUMENTS CAN STILL BE SEEN IN GREECE.

COTTON

RUINS OF DELPHI

GUARDIAN LION STATUES ON DELOS

ANCIENT GREEK VASE

LEMONS

IN THE 8TH CENTURY B.C., GREEKS CREATED A NETWORK OF COLONIES ALONG THE MEDITERRANEAN COAST AS FAR AS SPAIN.

ADRIATIC SEA

RUINS OF OLYMPIA

GREECE WAS A TURKISH PROVINCE FROM 1460 UNTIL 1827.

ROAD OF CORINTH

ATHENS

GREECE'S HEAVILY INDENTED COASTLINE IS 9,385 MILES LONG.

IONIAN SEA

ON A ROCKY HILL IN ATHENS, CALLED THE ACROPOLIS, SIT THE REMAINS OF A GROUP OF TEMPLES THE LARGEST AND MOST FAMOUS IS THE PARTHENON.

GREECE HAS ONE OF THE WORLD'S BIGGEST SHIPPING FLEETS.

TEMPLE OF ATHENA LINDIA AT LINDOS

RHODES

SHAKE MY HAND.

OCTOPUS

FEWER THAN 175 OF GREECE'S 2,000 ISLANDS ARE INHABITED.

SEA OF CRETE

WE ARE THE LARGEST GREEK ISLAND.

GREEK CULTURE WAS SPREAD ACROSS NORTH AFRICA AND ASIA BY ALEXANDER THE GREAT IN THE 4TH CENTURY B.C.

MEDITERRANEAN SEA

CRETE

RUINS OF KNOSSOS

DOLPHIN

ANCIENT GREEK SHIP

WE WERE ONCE THE CENTER OF THE MINOAN CIVILIZATION, WHICH FLOURISHED 3,500 YEARS AGO.

94